Calgary
Eats

Gail Norton
Karen Ralph

Calgary Eats

Signature Recipes
from the City's Best
Restaurants and Bars

Figure.1

Vancouver / Berkeley

GAIL NORTON

To Jean Norton, my mom and business partner for 22 years at The Cookbook Co. Cooks, who taught me how to prepare delicious food and the importance of gathering around a table with friends and family.

KAREN RALPH

For my parents, Bud and Norma Ralph, and my husband, Ian Grant, who's always supportive of my culinary projects.

Recipes are chef tested.

19 20 21 22 23 5 4 3 2 1

Cataloguing data is available from Library and Archives Canada
ISBN 978-1-77327-065-4 (hbk.)

Design by Jessica Sullivan
Photography by Chris Amat
Prop styling by Kaitlin Moerman

Editing by Michelle Meade
Copy editing by Judy Phillips
Proofreading by Breanne MacDonald
Indexing by Iva Cheung

Printed and bound in China by C&C Offset Printing Co., Ltd.
Distributed internationally by Publishers Group West

Figure 1 Publishing Inc.
Vancouver BC Canada
www.figure1publishing.com

Contents

Foreword

Over the past few decades, Calgary has evolved into one of the country's culinary hotspots, known for the talented chefs, butchers, bakers, bartenders, brewers and cheesemakers who make the best of what lives and grows here. It's a community built on relationships between chefs, growers and producers and inspired by our wheat, canola, barley and honey, beef, pork and bison, pulses and sugar beets.

Calgary is well within the realm of the world's best culinary destinations, a city where you can easily find delicious bread and pastries, spectacular wood-fired pizza and fresh pastas made with locally grown grains; fresh Vietnamese and Thai next door to smoky Argentinian barbecue and Indonesian restaurants serving up kati rolls, injera and *nasi goreng*. And in a province once synonymous with beef and steakhouses, some of our most celebrated restaurants make vegetables the star of the show.

Of course, all chefs rely on eaters. Our flourishing food community can largely be attributed to the food-savvy, adventurous and supportive Calgarians who appreciate great food and seek out unique culinary experiences from pop-ups, collaborations, markets and food trucks.

Although Calgary is home to thousands of eateries with a wide range of cultural backgrounds, the 40 restaurants that have contributed to this book are representations of Calgary's expansive culinary landscape. Locals go on the regular, and out-of-town visitors seek them out. The innovative recipes our talented chefs have shared in the following pages gently nudge the home cook into the realm of the restaurant kitchen, inspiring them with Alberta lamb, cold-pressed canola, asparagus and goat cheese, alongside imports like yuzu, olive oil, *gochujang* and calamansi limes. Although Calgary is a landlocked prairie city, our chefs demand fresh seafood be flown in daily, and fresh produce, spices and other ingredients are readily available at our shops and markets year-round.

Of course, food is inherently social; it brings people together around the table and facilitates conversation. And going out is a special occasion, whether the visit is celebratory or not. We dine at these restaurants, particularly the ones celebrated in this book, for the experience of trying something new or beyond our comfort zone. But those of us who love to cook look to these talented chefs and culinary professionals to inspire new and exciting dishes to make at home. After all, cooking is an experience in itself: a means of communication and creative outlet, and a way to reinforce relationships within our families and greater food community.

This collection of recipes reflects not only the range of ingredients we have access to here in Alberta but the cultural backgrounds and culinary skill of the chefs we're lucky enough to have feeding us. Thank you to all those who have shaped our culinary landscape and transformed the experiences they offer in their restaurants into this book, so that we may share their passion at our own dinner tables.

JULIE VAN ROSENDAAL

Introduction

When invited to participate in a cookbook celebrating the local culinary scene, the cooking community was incredibly supportive. And we realized something very quickly. Calgary's chefs want us to cook.

Calgary Eats is a celebration of the restaurant community gathering together. Enthusiastic chefs, bakers, brewers and bartenders contributed recipes, all in the spirit of showcasing dishes that would encourage more people to get into the kitchen, regardless of skill level, and make new discoveries about their food community—and best of all, have fun doing it.

We are thrilled to see many of those at restaurants featured in our first book, *Calgary Cooks*, returning to join a crop of new faces—and this collection of stalwarts, game changers and rising talents is a testament to how our food scene has evolved and grown. This benefits all of us who like to walk the streets, exploring markets and stores, looking for great food—we have it! Finding an exciting new restaurant is the kind of urban foraging we can all appreciate, and we've never eaten better.

Not that long ago, the only vegetarian item on a menu might be a humdrum salad or an uninspired pasta. Those days are over. Veggie-forward menus have gone mainstream, and now you can revel in exciting plant-based dishes such as Ten Foot Henry's Chargrilled Carrots with Salsa Verde, Avocado and Hazelnuts or The Coup's Wild Mushroom Dumplings with Celeriac Cream in the comforts of your own home.

We live in a city surrounded by grain fields, where a 20-minute drive takes you to cattle country. This connection to our land and its bounty has been inspiring chefs more than ever, and we are all the better for it. It makes sense: eating food grown close to home means being in sync with the seasons. It also brings an awareness of how tough the early settlers were, surviving through the winter on what they grew and raised. This attitude of endurance and making the best of what we've got lives on in the entrepreneurial spirits of our local chefs and restaurants; we no longer survive on cabbage soup, though Deane House gives us a delicious recipe for one (p. 83)!

Part of the fun of cooking is shopping for the ingredients. We encourage you to stroll the aisles of Asian supermarkets, Italian delis, specialty food stores and ethnic neighbourhood corner stores, where you are sure to always discover new foods and ingredients. And these discoveries might inspire new rituals of weekend trips to the farmers' markets and dinners in uncharted parts of town—as well as a new-found appreciation for (and addiction to—you've been warned) specialty food stores.

Some of the best moments in life are experienced around a table. Whether you're cooking recipes from *Calgary Eats* or taking a seat in one of the featured restaurants, you deserve to feel good about the way you spend your time. With these recipes, you can prepare delicious meals that can be shared with friends, helping build lasting memories.

One of the things we love most about Calgary is that our chefs are committed to keeping us constantly fed and inspired. We hope you enjoy this book as much as we enjoyed putting it together for you. From our restaurants to your homes: Cook, eat, be happy!

KAREN AND GAIL

The
Restaurants

The Recipes

15

Alloy Dining
Rogelio Herrera

Moreover, Alloy has an excellent in-house catering program and, with a beautiful pergola-covered patio, surrounded by a rock garden and bestowed with plenty of comfortable seating, it is a popular venue for exchanging vows.

ABOUT THE CHEF

Chef and co-owner Rogelio Herrera spent most of his life working in restaurants. He started as a dishwasher, moved up to line cook and eventually became the "pasta guy." From there, he worked as sous chef in some of Calgary's leading restaurants before opening Alloy with Uri Heilik. He's experienced both the challenges and triumphs of owning a restaurant and has learned what works and what doesn't.

In addition to running the restaurant, Herrera has partnered with SAIT (Southern Alberta Institute of Technology) to offer work experience for culinary students at his kitchen. The students, ranging in age from 18 to 25, spend a few hours in the kitchen and a few hours in front of house. At the end of the day, they sit down to dinner with Herrera. This dedication to helping young people change their lives through work and education proves that one can lead by example and make the world a better place through kindness, compassion and excellent food. "It's been 11 years and I still can't believe it," Herrera shares. "Every day that I wake up to work at Alloy is like a beautiful dream."

Alloy, in Manchester Industrial, may be off the beaten path, but that hasn't stopped hungry Calgarians from flocking to the restaurant in droves. Elegant design and warm lighting add an understated glamour to the room, but the real highlight is the excellent food, thanks to the talented chef Rogelio Herrera.

The inventive cooking has a firm foundation in continental cuisine but takes bold flavour forays into Latin America and Asia. Creations such as beef short rib croquettes with herbed aioli and serrano pepper oil, and pork tenderloin in a tamarind reduction, served with vanilla cauliflower purée, bok choy and compressed pears keep patrons very happy. The menu changes twice a year (with full input from his kitchen crew), and the carefully curated wine list by business partner Uri Heilik always complements.

Pickled mangoes
- 2 mangoes, peeled, pitted and finely chopped
- 2 Tbsp granulated sugar
- 1 tsp kosher salt
- 1 tsp gochugaru or red chili flakes
- Juice of 1 lemon

Citrus dressing
- ½ cup mayonnaise
- ½ cup full-fat sour cream
- 1 tsp ground turmeric
- Juice of 1 orange
- Juice of 1 lemon
- Juice of 1 lime
- Kosher salt, to taste

Togarashi tuna
- ¼ cup togarashi
- 1 (24-oz) tuna centre loin, sliced into eight 3-oz pieces
- 2 Tbsp grapeseed oil
- Kosher salt, to taste

Assembly
- 1 head Romaine lettuce, halved lengthwise and core removed, cut into thin strips
- 16 small tomatoes, halved
- Chili oil, for garnish (optional)

Seared Albacore Tuna, Pickled Mango, Romaine, Citrus Dressing

Serves 8

This well-balanced recipe has the right amount of crunch with Romaine, spice with *togarashi* (a Japanese spice blend of spicy pepper, sesame seeds and dried orange peel) and sweetness with the mango and the citrus dressing. Togarashi can be found at any Asian supermarket. The pickled mangoes can be made ahead and kept in the refrigerator. They are super delicious with chicken or pork recipes or as a snack on yogurt—so good!

Pickled mangoes In a bowl, combine all ingredients. Cover and refrigerate until needed. (You can leave them for at least 1 week, but they're best if used within 2 days.)

Citrus dressing In a mixing bowl, combine mayonnaise, sour cream and turmeric. Add citrus juices and season with salt. Refrigerate until needed.

Togarashi tuna Place togarashi in a shallow bowl and dredge tuna in it to thoroughly coat. Place tuna on a large plate or baking sheet.

Heat oil in a frying pan over medium heat until nearly smoking. Add tuna and sear for 10 seconds on each side, or until cooked rare (still red) on the inside. Transfer tuna to a plate lined with paper towel to drain any excess fat. Sprinkle with salt to taste.

Set aside to cool, then slice each portion into 3 equal slices.

Assembly In a large bowl, combine lettuce and dressing and season with more salt.

Divide salad among eight plates. Place 3 slices of tuna on top of salad. Place pickled mango alongside each slice of tuna. Garnish with tomatoes and a drizzle of chili oil, if using.

Flourless chocolate cake
7 oz dark chocolate
¾ cup (1½ sticks) unsalted butter, plus extra for greasing
1 Tbsp gochugaru
3 eggs
3 egg yolks
1 cup granulated sugar
1 tsp vanilla extract
¼ cup sifted cocoa powder
Mint, for garnish (optional)
Edible flowers, for garnish (optional)

Chantilly cream
½ vanilla bean, halved lengthwise
1 cup heavy cream
½ cup icing sugar
½ tsp vanilla extract

Macerated berries
1 cup strawberries, halved
1 cup blueberries
1 cup blackberries
1 cup raspberries
⅓ cup dark rum
Juice of 1 lemon
½ cup icing sugar
1 tsp kosher salt

Flourless Chocolate Cake with Chantilly Cream and Macerated Berries

Serves 8

Chocolate, cream and berries bring out the best in each other but this cake gets star treatment with the addition of *gochugaru*—Korean chili flakes. Gochugaru can be found at Asian supermarkets.

Flourless chocolate cake Preheat oven to 350°F.

Lightly grease a 9- × 13-inch baking sheet with a lip.

Using a double boiler, melt chocolate and butter, stirring to combine. Add gochugaru. Remove from heat and allow to cool slightly.

In a large bowl, whisk eggs, egg yolks, sugar and vanilla. Whisking continuously, slowly pour in the chocolate mixture. Add cocoa powder and mix well.

Pour the batter onto the prepared baking sheet and bake for 15 minutes, or until cooked through. (Keep an eye on the cake—it's easy to burn.) Remove from oven and set aside for 20 minutes to cool. Refrigerate, uncovered, for at least 2 hours or overnight. (The cake can be stored in the refrigerator, covered, for up to 5 days.)

Chantilly cream Using the flat side of a knife, scrape the vanilla seeds into a large bowl. Discard pod. Pour in heavy cream, then add icing sugar and vanilla extract. Using an electric mixer, whip at medium-high speed for 3 minutes, or until soft peaks form. Cover with plastic wrap and chill until serving.

Macerated berries Combine berries and rum in a large mixing bowl. Add lemon juice, sugar and salt and mix well. Cover and refrigerate until needed. (Do not prepare this too far in advance or the fruit will lose its texture.)

Assembly Remove the cake from the refrigerator. Cut into squares and place on the serving plate. Bring to room temperature and add a generous spoonful of macerated berries and a dollop (or two or three) of Chantilly cream. Garnish each cake with mint and edible flowers, if using. Serve immediately.

The Block Kitchen and Lounge
Mike Preston

be a serious error. Why? Simply put: The Block serves up a stellar combination of satisfying, familiar food and generous portions—what could be better?

ABOUT THE CHEF

"I learn something new—good or bad—from everyone I work with."

Originally influenced by his grandmother, whose colourful advice was quotable but not printable, Chef Mike Preston quickly learned at the age of 15 that a professional kitchen would be his second home. Born and raised in Alberta, he graduated from SAIT's (Southern Alberta Institute of Technology's) Cook Apprentice program, building his career in hotels, country clubs and fine-dining restaurants in Calgary. With rustic dishes such as the salumi board—consisting of cured meats, artisanal cheeses and olives—or lamb sirloin with mashed potatoes, his concise market-led dishes are influenced by the flavours of Italy and Canadian-grown and -produced products.

Located in Mount Pleasant, The Block Kitchen and Lounge serves comfort food at its best. It's a cozy space with warm wood interior accents, a lounge with big screens for watching the latest game and a dining room with an often-sun-drenched patio. On any given night, you might see groups of friends and families sharing plates of chicken wings, crispy calamari, capicollo pizza and cheese-stuffed arancini. Staff are friendly, the vibe is fun. No wonder it's been hailed as one of the best restaurants in the neighbourhood.

And while this restaurant serves meals from dusk to dawn, it's the dinner menu that shines: we're talking pastas, perfectly cooked Angus beef and pork tenderloin stuffed with pecan, basil and apple. In fact, to leave here without ordering the Nico pizza or the cheesecake would

Poached beets

12 large red beets, unpeeled
1 bay leaf
1 Tbsp black peppercorns
1 Tbsp fennel seeds

Pickled beets

6 Poached Beets (see here), peeled and cut into ¼-inch-thick slices
4 cups red wine vinegar
2 cups granulated sugar
2 star anise
1 bay leaf
2 Tbsp yellow mustard seeds

Beet dressing

½ star anise
1 Poached Beet (see here), coarsely chopped
1 Tbsp honey
3 Tbsp white wine vinegar
¼ cup canola or olive oil
Kosher salt and freshly ground black pepper, to taste

Candied pecans

½ cup (1 stick) unsalted butter, melted
3 large egg whites
1 cup granulated sugar
1 tsp ground cinnamon
4 cups pecan halves

Assembly

3 cups baby arugula
4 oz goat cheese

Serves 6

"Eat to the Beet" Salad

Sweet, densely flavoured beets have been called the "thug" of the vegetable world. This dish showcases beets three ways—pickled, poached and puréed into a vinaigrette—and pairs them with the caramel crunch of candied pecans.

Poached beets Place the ingredients in a large saucepan, add enough water to completely cover and boil for 1 hour, or until beets are easily pierced with a sharp knife. Drain, then set aside on a plate to cool.

Once cool enough to handle, peel 5 beets and slice into ¼-inch rounds. Set aside. Set aside 7 beets for later.

Pickled beets Put beets in a bowl.

In a large saucepan, combine the remaining ingredients, add 2 litres water and bring to a boil. Cook for 3 minutes, or until fragrant and sugar is dissolved. Strain the liquid, reserving the vinegar mixture but discarding the spices.

Pour the hot vinegar mixture over the sliced beets and cover the bowl with plastic wrap, piercing the wrap with the tip of a sharp knife to create steam vents. Refrigerate until beets

have cooled completely. These will keep in the fridge for up to 2 weeks.

Beet dressing Using a mortar and pestle, crush star anise into a coarse powder.

In a blender, purée beet, star anise, honey and vinegar to a paste. With the motor still running, slowly add oil until mixture is emulsified. Season with salt and pepper.

Candied pecans Preheat oven to 350°F. Line a large baking sheet with parchment paper. In a large bowl, combine butter, egg whites, sugar and cinnamon. Add pecans and toss to thoroughly coat. Spread pecans on the baking sheet. Bake for 30 minutes, stirring pecans every 10 minutes. Remove from oven and set aside to cool for 10 to 15 minutes.

Assembly On a platter, pile sliced poached beets on one side and arrange a row of pickled beets beside it. In a bowl, toss arugula with dressing, then place in the centre of the platter.

Sprinkle candied pecans over arugula and top with loosely crumbled goat cheese. Serve family-style.

2 cups sliced cured sausage

¼ cup extra-virgin olive oil, plus extra for frying

¼ cup (½ stick) unsalted butter

1 onion, thinly sliced

1 red bell pepper, seeded, deveined and cut into thin strips

1 fennel bulb, cored and cut into thin strips

4 cloves garlic, finely chopped

1 cup dry white wine

16 tiger prawns, peeled and deveined

1 lb tagliatelle pasta

Kosher salt and freshly ground black pepper, to taste

½ cup grated Parmesan

1 heaping Tbsp finely chopped Italian parsley

Serves 4

Prawn and Sausage Tagliatelle

Prawns and sausages are found paired together in dishes the world over, and the combo is magical. This recipe is made with a cured Hungarian sausage, but feel free to substitute your favourite cured sausage.

Heat a generous splash of oil in a large frying pan. Add sausage and cook for 10 minutes, or until slightly brown and cooked through. Transfer to a plate and set aside.

Heat ¼ cup oil and butter in the same pan over medium heat. Add onion, bell pepper, fennel and garlic and cook for 10 to 15 minutes, until vegetables are softened and onion is translucent.

Meanwhile, bring a large pot of salted water to a boil.

Add sausage and any juices that have collected on the plate to the pan of vegetables, pour in wine and bring to a boil. Reduce heat to medium-low and simmer for 10 minutes, or until the sauce is reduced and has thickened.

Add pasta to the pot of water and cook according to package instructions until al dente. Drain.

Assembly Add prawns to the frying pan with the sausage mixture and cook for 4 minutes, or until pink, opaque and cooked through. (Do not overcook.)

Place pasta in a deep serving platter and top with sauce. Season with salt and pepper. Sprinkle with Parmesan and parsley and serve.

Bow Valley Ranche Restaurant

Jenny M. Kang

Gull Valley Greenhouse tomatoes to Brant Lake wagyu striploin.

Bow Valley Ranche is a consummate crowd-pleaser. Chef Jenny Kang's carefully crafted menu is full of elegant dishes made with calculated precision: from Bouvry Farm elk tartare to pan-seared Pacific halibut to Rougié confit duck leg.

ABOUT THE CHEF

Jenny M. Kang, who joined the Bow Valley Ranche team in 2015, strives to create menus with quality, sustainability and local ingredients. The chef grew up on a farm in South Korea, and those formative years taught her about food provenance and the values of cooking seasonally. It also shaped her approach to cooking and to leading a strong team.

"Watching vegetables grown from seed to harvest, raising animals and cooking gave me a true understanding of food and flavour and a strong knowledge of nutrition," Kang tells us. "These experiences inspire my cooking today, and I always want to create unique dishes with an emphasis on local, sustainable ingredients. After all, cooking food creates love and happiness." We couldn't agree with her more.

Bow Valley Ranche Restaurant in Fish Creek Park has been a long-time favourite for celebrating special occasions. In 1902, this magnificent and historic ranch house was owned by Senator Patrick Burns, a man renowned for hosting events and welcoming friends. His company logo was made up of an "N" and a backwards "L," which meant that his doors were "never locked."

So when Great Events Catering took over the space in 2013, it preserved the tradition of hospitality. Known for its locally sourced Canadian cuisine, the restaurant takes advantage of the freshest and tastiest ingredients from the area and boasts a menu that celebrates local producers native to the Canadian Rockies. Sustainability is the name of the game, and regional ingredients include everything from

Yuzu vinaigrette

½ cup freshly squeezed yuzu juice
  or combination of citrus juices

3 Tbsp grapeseed or olive oil

2 Tbsp granulated sugar

½ tsp Dijon mustard

Albacore tuna crudo

1 lb high-quality Albacore tuna
  loin or salmon

3 radishes, thinly sliced

½ cucumber, finely chopped

½ Granny Smith apple, cut into
  matchsticks

Broccoli sprouts, for garnish

Maldon salt, to taste

Serves 6

Albacore Tuna Crudo

The history of food is the history of travel. Here, Japan meets Italy and the result is Italian sashimi. To make this impressive dish, you'll need sushi-grade tuna, which can be found at North Sea Fish Market in Willow Park and Meta4 Foods at 903B 48th Avenue SE. Yuzu, a Japanese citrus fruit, is complex in flavour. Buy yuzu at The Cookbook Co. Cooks (p. 62) or substitute a combination of citrus juices, such as lemon, lime and grapefruit.

Yuzu vinaigrette In a bowl, combine all ingredients and whisk until the sugar dissolves. Set aside.

Albacore tuna crudo Slice the tuna (or salmon) into ½-inch cubes and refrigerate until needed.

Combine radishes, cucumber and apple in a bowl and set aside.

Assembly Divide the tuna (or salmon) into 6 equal portions and place in the centre of six individual plates. Top each with equal amounts of radish salad.

Drizzle yuzu vinaigrette overtop and dress to your taste. (Leftover vinaigrette can be stored in a sealed jar for up to 6 days.) Garnish with broccoli sprouts and Maldon salt. Serve immediately.

▶ Ricotta Gnocchi with Confit Duck Leg
and Mushrooms | p. 28

Confit duck legs

4 duck legs

½ cup kosher salt

2 heads garlic, separated into
   cloves and peeled

3 sprigs thyme

5 bay leaves

20 black peppercorns

5 cups melted duck fat

Ricotta gnocchi

2 egg yolks

2 cups ricotta

1 tsp kosher salt

2½ cups all-purpose flour (divided),
   plus extra for dusting

1 Tbsp extra-virgin olive oil

Creamy mushroom sauce

3 Tbsp grapeseed oil

2 cups sliced assorted mushrooms

1 shallot, finely chopped

2 whole heads roasted garlic
   (see Confit Duck Leg here)

¼ cup white wine

2 cups whipping cream

3½ to 4 cups baby arugula

½ tsp kosher salt

Ricotta Gnocchi with Confit Duck Leg and Mushrooms

Serves 4

The gnocchi are tossed with mushroom sauce and confit duck and garnished with crunchy, crispy duck skin—this is next-level comfort food that makes for an elegant dinner. You'll need to start your preparations a day in advance, so if you're short on time, purchase pre-made duck confit from a specialty food store. The mushroom sauce can also be prepared in advance and heated through when ready to serve.

Confit duck legs Place duck legs, skin side down, in a roasting pan large enough to fit the legs without them touching. Salt the top of the legs, cover and refrigerate overnight.

Preheat oven to 220°F.

Rinse duck legs under cold running water. Place them back in a roasting pan, skin side up, and add garlic, thyme, bay leaves and peppercorns. Pour in duck fat to completely submerge legs. Roast for 3 hours, or until the meat is tender and almost falling off the bone. Remove pan from oven and set aside until cool enough to handle, then transfer duck legs to a plate.

Strain duck fat into resealable containers. Store, sealed, in the refrigerator for up to 6 months. The duck fat can be used to roast meats and vegetables or for your next batch of confit.

Pull the meat and skin off the bones, then separate the skin from the meat. Set the skin aside. Pull the duck meat into large pieces and place in a bowl. Discard the bones. Reserve garlic for mushroom sauce.

In a frying pan over medium heat, fry duck skin until very crispy. Transfer to a plate lined with paper towel and set aside.

Ricotta gnocchi In a large bowl, mix egg yolks, ricotta and salt to thoroughly combine. Add 2 cups flour to bring mixture together into a dough. Use the remaining ½ cup to lightly flour a work surface. Gently knead the dough on the floured work surface until it just forms a ball. Adding a little flour at a time, work into a soft dough. (You might not need to add the full amount.) Place dough in the bowl and set aside at room temperature to rest for 1 hour.

Shaved or grated Parmesan,
    for garnish
1 tsp truffle oil or fresh truffle
    shavings

NOTE: If you'd like to freeze the gnocchi, place them on a baking sheet lined with parchment paper and freeze for 2 hours, or until completely frozen. Store in resealable bags. To thaw, place on a parchment-lined, floured baking sheet. Do not thaw (even a little bit) the gnocchi in the resealable bag or they will stick together and revert to a ball of dough! When ready to serve, cook the gnocchi from frozen for 8 minutes, or until they float to the surface.

Line a baking sheet with parchment paper and generously cover with flour.

Roll the dough into a ½-inch-thick rope and cut evenly into ¾-inch segments. Place pieces on the prepared baking sheet and toss in flour. (Add more flour, if necessary, to prevent them from sticking to each other.)

Bring a large saucepan of salted water to a boil. Add gnocchi and cook for 4 minutes, or until they float to the surface. Drain and transfer gnocchi to a bowl. Toss with oil to prevent sticking and set aside.

Creamy mushroom sauce Heat oil in a large frying pan. Add mushrooms and shallot and sauté for 15 minutes, or until water has been released and they begin to brown. Add roasted garlic and pour in wine, scraping the bottom of the pan to release any browned bits. Stir in cream and cook for 5 minutes, or until sauce is thick enough to coat the back of a spoon. Add arugula to the pan, toss and cook for 1 minute. Season with salt.

Assembly Stir gnocchi and duck confit pieces into mushroom sauce, then transfer to individual plates or bowls. Garnish with Parmesan, a drizzle of truffle oil (or truffle shavings) and crushed crispy duck skin. Serve immediately.

Bread and Circus Trattoria
Kayle Burns

without even realizing what you're missing. We recommend you take a seat in the dining room or at the chef's bar: the kitchen is on full display, all the better to watch the chef and his team at work. Start with one of the restaurant's popular aperitifs and settle in for the evening.

ABOUT THE CHEF

Executive chef Kayle Burns oversees the menus for both UNA Pizza + Wine (p. 196) and Bread and Circus. Originally from Quebec, Burns discovered his passion and talent for cooking in Switzerland and has since trained in New York, Tokyo, Melbourne and Sydney. Today, he calls Calgary home. His cooking is a celebration of local, simple food and our community, whether he's preparing a batch of homemade apple cider vinegar (to serve with cauliflower salad) or working with local urban farmers to cultivate quality produce. From the heightened presentation of his dishes to the time he spends away from the kitchen in order to interact with the diners, Burns's commitment to food and hospitality is clear.

If Juvenal's words are anything to go by, you'll be back for more.

Roman satirist Juvenal once proclaimed that "two things only the people anxiously desire—bread and circuses" (meaning that the government was controlling the population, and its votes, with food and entertainment). The phrase became the inspiration for Bread and Circus Trattoria.

Located off 17th Avenue SW, the small restaurant isn't visible from the street. You enter through UNA Takeaway and, like a delicious secret, there it is. This cozy restaurant is inspired by the convivial trattorias of Rome, serving up a menu that is "dictated by custom and comfort." More than that, it's fun to discover a spot that you might have walked past a hundred times

Salt cod

1 lb salt cod
1¼ cups extra-virgin olive oil
Crusty baguette, sliced, to serve

Crushed olive oil potatoes

12 new potatoes, unpeeled
2 tsp kosher salt
¼ cup extra-virgin olive oil
2 Tbsp chopped capers
2 Tbsp finely chopped Italian parsley
Grated zest and juice of 2 lemons
Sprigs of dill or oregano, for garnish

Salt Cod and Crushed Olive Oil Potatoes

Serves 6 to 8

Salt cod is a staple dish in many sea-bound parts of the world, and this dish reminds us of what all the fuss is about. The cured fish needs to rehydrate in cold water for 1 to 2 days. The dish can be served warm or, if you like, at room temperature—simply skip the 20 minutes of baking and instead just mix, garnish and serve with a simple salad.

Salt cod Rinse salt cod under cold running water, then place in a large bowl. Add enough cold water to cover it. Refrigerate for 24 hours, changing the water four times. Drain and set aside, then pat dry with paper towel.

Heat oil in a small saucepan over medium heat until the oil reaches a temperature of 155°F. Add cod and poach on a low simmer for 20 minutes, or until the cod flakes apart. Using a slotted spoon, transfer fish to a plate lined with paper towel. Remove any bones, then break cod into large chunks and set aside.

Crushed olive oil potatoes Preheat oven to 375°F.

Put potatoes in a medium saucepan, add enough water to cover and bring to a boil. Add salt, reduce heat to medium and simmer for 15 to 20 minutes, until potatoes are tender. Drain and set aside to cool.

Place potatoes on a baking sheet and, using the side of a large knife, smash each to break the skin. Transfer to a baking dish, add cod and gently mix. Add oil, capers, parsley, lemon zest and three-quarters of the lemon juice. Bake for 20 minutes, or until potatoes are slightly brown. Set aside and let cool to room temperature.

Garnish with herbs, sprinkle with the remaining lemon juice and serve with sliced baguette.

6 oz pancetta, diced
Olive oil (optional)
2 large cloves garlic, chopped
1 tsp red chili flakes
2 cups San Marzano passata
1 lb bigoli pasta
½ cup grated or shaved pecorino
Crusty bread, sliced, to serve

Serves 4

Bigoli all'Amatriciana

Here, magnificent pancetta adds a depth of flavour to this classic spicy pasta dish. If you've never tried bigoli, now is the time. Bigoli, a type of pasta particularly popular in Rome, is made with hard durum wheat flour and looks like thick spaghetti, which is perfect for absorbing sauce. The passata—strained tomato—is the basis of the sauce and can be found in larger supermarkets.

Heat a large frying pan over medium heat, add the pancetta and cook for 5 minutes, or until golden brown. (If pancetta is on the lean side, add a splash of olive oil.) Transfer to a plate and set aside.

In the same pan with the fat, add garlic and chili flakes and sauté for 1 to 2 minutes over medium heat, until fragrant. Add passata, reduce heat to medium-low and simmer for 10 minutes.

Meanwhile, bring a large pot of salted water to a boil. Add bigoli and cook for 10 minutes, or until it's about 80% cooked. (It should still be firm.) Drain, then add to sauce and cook for another 5 minutes, or until al dente. (We always finish cooking our pasta this way because it makes the sauce stick to it.)

Transfer pasta to a serving platter and garnish with pecorino and the crispy pancetta. Serve with crusty bread and a rustic red wine.

Bridgette Bar
JP Pedhirney

When you think you've tried and tasted every dining concept that Calgary has to offer, think again. Bridgette Bar has taken on the art of cooking over an open flame to the next level. St. Brigid (the goddess of fire in Irish mythology) inspired the concept of open-flame cookery, and at the heart of this relaxed and cozy two-level restaurant is a wood-burning hearth, which sees farm-fresh chicken and duck or fresh fish like halibut chargrilled over embers—it's a treat to watch the chefs and furnaces in action.

And let's talk about that space. Exposed ceilings and brick walls? Check. Double-height ceiling? Check. How about antique doors, banquette tables and macramé? Check, check, check. While the cooking may have been inspired by ancient folklore, the bar itself is a tribute to the legendary Brigitte Bardot and her joie de vivre.

General manager Dewey Noordhof, a long-time restaurateur, welcomes guests at the door. Food, wine and beer lists are changed frequently—sometimes twice a month—ensuring a satisfying, seasonal meal in an open yet intimate room.

ABOUT THE CHEF

Executive chef JP Pedhirney's vision of a restaurant devoted to hearth cooking was made a reality thanks to hard work, experience and the team at Concorde Entertainment Group that supported his vision. After earning his Red Seal certificate, he worked at River Café (p. 164) and then trained at the Michelin-starred Blackbird in Chicago. He returned to Calgary to work as sous chef at Rouge Restaurant and quickly became chef de cuisine.

Pedhirney sources the best ethically raised meats and local produce to create an ever-changing seasonal menu and shows that hearth-cooked meals create a sense of shared community. "I like the versatility of hearth cooking," Pedhirney shares. "It's gentle, and the distinct aroma of the wood fire instantly evokes comfort."

▷ Grilled Asparagus with Burrata, Calamansi Dressing and Sourdough Croutons | p. 36

Asparagus

1 bunch asparagus, trimmed

Calamansi dressing

2 Tbsp calamansi vinegar

2 tsp white wine vinegar

3 Tbsp canola oil

2 tsp extra-virgin olive oil

½ tsp kosher salt

Sourdough croutons

2 Tbsp unsalted butter

2 cloves garlic

1 sprig thyme

4 cups cubed sourdough, with crust

Assembly

Vegetable oil, for coating

Kosher salt and freshly ground black pepper, to taste

1 ball burrata, to serve

Good-quality olive oil

Grilled Asparagus with Burrata, Calamansi Dressing and Sourdough Croutons

Serves 4

There's a saying that the best inheritance is an asparagus patch. Grilled and topped with creamy burrata, chewy croutons and tart, zesty calamansi dressing, this salad fully embodies raw spring power. Calamansi is kumquat-orange hybrid fruit with an intense citrus flavour. You can replace it with a mixture of equal amounts lemon, orange and rice vinegar.

Asparagus Bring a large pot of salted water to a boil.

Meanwhile, use your fingers to snap off the bottom of each asparagus spear. (The stems naturally break where the tough, woody part ends and the tender stem begins.)

Fill a large bowl with ice water and set aside. Place asparagus in the boiling water and cook for 30 to 90 seconds, until the stems turn bright green. Using tongs, transfer asparagus to the bowl of ice water. Drain and set aside.

Calamansi dressing In a Mason jar or other lidded container, combine all ingredients, then add 1 tablespoon water. Shake well to mix and refrigerate until needed. (Shake again before using.)

Sourdough croutons Melt butter in a large frying pan over medium heat until it begins to foam. Add garlic and thyme and cook for 30 seconds. Add sourdough and cook, stirring occasionally, for 5 minutes, or until golden. Turn off the heat.

Using a spoon, transfer the croutons to a plate lined with paper towel and set aside to drain for 10 minutes. Store in a sealed container at room temperature until needed.

Assembly Preheat the grill or barbecue. Combine asparagus and vegetable oil in a bowl and lightly season with salt and pepper.

Place asparagus on the grill crosswise to avoid the spears falling through the grates. Gently roll asparagus for 2 to 3 minutes to develop an even char. Transfer asparagus to a baking sheet. Drizzle half of the calamansi dressing overtop, reserving leftover dressing for a later use.

Arrange asparagus on a serving platter. Spoon over calamansi dressing until the bottom of the platter is lightly covered. Place ball of burrata on top or tear into pieces and place them randomly over the asparagus. Scatter croutons overtop. Finish with a drizzle of olive oil and a sprinkle of salt and pepper.

Pictured | p. 35

Bean ragout
2 cups dried cannellini beans
1 white onion, halved
1 bay leaf
½ tsp kosher salt
1 Tbsp sherry vinegar

Green chili purée
2 green Thai chilies, seeded
  and stems removed
1 stalk lemongrass, white part only,
  finely chopped
2 cups packed spinach
⅓ cup reserved bean-cooking liquid
  (see Bean Ragout)
¼ cup Bean Ragout (see here)
2 tsp finely chopped ginger
1 tsp coriander seeds
1 tsp kosher salt

Segmented grapefruit
1 grapefruit

Roasted halibut
4 (6-oz) halibut fillets
Kosher salt
3 Tbsp olive oil
4 oz canned Dungeness
  crabmeat

Roasted Halibut with Chilies, Dungeness Crab, Bean Ragout and Grapefruit

Serves 4

Calgary might be landlocked, but Calgarians love fish! This hearty yet nuanced dish is a marriage of rich flavours that are brightened up by grapefruit. The beans require overnight soaking, so start a day in advance.

Bean ragout Soak beans in a bowl of cold water overnight. The next day, drain water.

Put beans, onion and bay leaf in a large saucepan, then add enough water to cover beans by 1 inch. Simmer over medium-high heat for 60 to 90 minutes, until beans are tender. (Add more water, if necessary, to keep the beans submerged.) To keep beans intact, the water must simmer and not vigorously boil. Turn off the heat and stir in salt and vinegar. Set aside for 1 hour, or until cooled.

Discard onion and bay leaf. Strain liquid from beans, reserving both.

Green chili purée In a food processor or blender, purée all ingredients together on high speed until smooth. Refrigerate.

Segmented grapefruit Using a sharp knife, cut the top and bottom of the grapefruit, making large enough cuts that the flesh is exposed. The grapefruit should sit solidly on the cutting board.

Starting at the top of the grapefruit, cut downward, following the contour of the fruit and cutting out the peel and white pith of the peel. Once this step is complete, the grapefruit should be whole, without peel or pith, and the flesh completely exposed.

Holding the grapefruit in one hand, carefully cut in between the membrane to release segments. Trim any excess white pith (as this can be bitter). Cut each segment in half lengthwise and set aside.

Roasted halibut Preheat oven to 350°F.

Pat fillets dry, then generously sprinkle with salt.

Heat oil in an ovenproof or cast-iron frying pan over high heat until nearly smoking. Add fillets, taking care not to splash the hot oil, and cook for 30 seconds. Place pan in the oven and cook for 5 minutes, or until the centre of the fish is warmed through and the thickest part has an internal temperature between 135°F and 145°F. (Do not overcook.)

Assembly In a saucepan, combine the remaining beans and chili purée and gently warm over medium heat until mixture thickens to a porridge-like consistency. (If necessary, add reserved bean liquid to thin it out.) Stir in crabmeat and season with salt.

Spoon crab ragout into the centre of a serving platter. Using an offset spatula, carefully place fillets on top. Garnish with grapefruit segments and serve.

The Bro'Kin Yolk
Jeff and Gil Carlos

The name says it all.

Brothers Jeff and Gil Carlos, seeing a gap in the restaurant scene, combined their 20 years of restaurant experience to create a cozy and affordable farm-to-table dining spot for suburbanites. The simple stripped-back interior is unpretentious and comfortable, complementing their style of cooking.

The menu offers comfort fare for everyone, but sometimes we find it hard to choose, because it's all so good: chicken and waffles, frittatas, poutines and even a few surprises, such as the Bro's Breakfast, a pork belly adobo dish that represents the brothers' Filipino heritage. They even have a solid selection "For the Littles."

Best of all, The Bro'Kin Yolk offers a stress-free brunch experience. Simply call ahead to have them text you when your table is ready. And there's always plenty of parking. This is stress-free dining that won't blow the budget and possibly might convince you never to cook breakfast or lunch at home again. The brothers have already opened a second location, in Mahogany, and are set to diversify with a takeout place called Bro's To Go. "We wanted to own a restaurant that gave us more flexibility with our schedules so we could also spend evenings at home with our families," says Gil. "A breakfast/brunch restaurant made this possible."

The family-oriented restaurant feels like home, and it's the type of place to return to time and again.

ABOUT THE CHEFS

Jeff and Gil Carlos are the bros behind The Bro'Kin Yolk. Jeff runs the kitchen and back of house, and Gil manages the front of house. With a Red Seal certificate, Jeff dreamt of owning a food truck, whereas Gil was heading for the corporate world. When the brothers realized that the suburbs were in desperate need of a decent breakfast spot, they took the opportunity to team up, investing in brick-and-mortar. And luckily for brunch-obsessed Calgarians, Bro'Kin Yolk was born.

"Breakfast is when I get to spend time with my family before the day gets crazy," explains Jeff. "So I cherish these peaceful memories."

½ cup soy sauce

3 Tbsp granulated sugar

2 Tbsp brown sugar

2 Tbsp liquid smoke

1 Tbsp paprika

1 Tbsp kosher salt

1 lb pork belly, sliced to desired
   thickness

Serves 4

House-Cured Bacon

Tocino is a sweet cured meat made from pork belly and typically served just like bacon in Filipino breakfasts and lunch. The Carlos brothers have personalized this popular traditional recipe with a few original tweaks, elevating a Filipino breakfast staple to something even more delicious. The brothers prefer Bon Ton Meat Market's pork belly, but you can also purchase it at Italian Centre, Empire Provisions (p. 96) and Asian supermarkets.

In a large bowl, combine all ingredients except pork belly. Pour in ½ cup water and whisk until thoroughly combined. Add pork belly and mix well, then cover and refrigerate for at least 4 hours but preferably overnight.

Drain off excess marinade and pat pork belly dry with paper towel. Heat a frying pan over medium heat and pan-fry pork belly for 4 minutes on each side, or until cooked through. Cook it slightly longer if you want it crispier. (Alternatively, bake in a preheated oven at 375°F for 15 to 20 minutes.) Set aside to cool. The pork belly can be stored in a glass or plastic container for up to 1 week.

Enjoy as a side with your favourite meals, crumbled over salads or as a savoury, satisfying snack.

Pork belly
4 cloves garlic
3 bay leaves
1 cup soy sauce
1 cup white vinegar
1 Tbsp freshly squeezed lemon juice
1 Tbsp freshly ground black pepper
1 lb pork belly, cut into 1-inch chunks

Salsa
1 Roma tomato, chopped
1 green onion, thinly sliced
½ red onion, finely chopped
1 Tbsp freshly squeezed lemon juice
1½ tsp kosher salt
1½ tsp freshly ground black pepper

Rice
1 cup jasmine rice,
   thoroughly rinsed

Assembly
2 Tbsp canola oil (divided)
4 eggs

Serves 2

The Bro's Breakfast

The Bro's Breakfast is based on what is arguably the Philippines' most popular dish thanks to its bold, simple flavours. Here, the brothers have ramped up their mom's traditional recipe—with spectacular results.

Pork belly In a medium bowl, combine garlic, bay leaves, soy sauce, vinegar, lemon juice and pepper. Add pork belly and mix well, then cover and refrigerate for at least 4 hours but preferably overnight.

Salsa In a small bowl, combine all ingredients and set aside. Don't make this too far in advance or the tomatoes will turn mushy.

Rice In a saucepan, combine rice and 1½ cups water, cover and bring to a boil. Reduce heat to medium-low and simmer for 30 minutes, or until cooked through. Remove from heat and set aside for 15 minutes to steam.

Assembly Drain pork belly and pat dry with paper towel. Discard marinade.

Heat 1 tablespoon oil in a frying pan over medium heat. Carefully add pork belly and sear each side for 5 minutes, or until browned. Reduce heat to medium-low, cover and fry on low for 15 minutes.

Once the pork is nearly done, heat the remaining 1 tablespoon oil in a separate frying pan and fry eggs to desired doneness.

Place pork on individual plates, add rice and salsa and place a fried egg on the side. Any leftover pork can be kept refrigerated in a glass or plastic container for up to 1 week.

Calcutta Cricket Club
Rene Bhullar

But it's the standout Indian food that is truly at the heart of this restaurant, where regional dishes represent history and waves of migrant-influenced and family traditions. And it's here where you'll find well-executed small plates that are authentic renderings of Kolkata and West Bengali food, with many vegetarian choices.

"We're constantly looking to preserve authentic dishes while allowing our chefs to express their creativity," explains Sengupta. "The popular Bengali adage 'What Bengal thinks today, India thinks tomorrow' speaks to the region's progressive thinking and vision. Our goal is to always think outside the box and present dishes that aren't typically found in Indian restaurants."

ABOUT THE CHEF

For many years, Rene Bhullar was a chemist with a passion for cooking. However, in 2012, he pursued his dream and put on chef's whites for his first culinary job at Cilantro (p. 56). Bhullar then worked at Cucina and Ox Bar de Tapas (formerly Ox & Angela), before moving to Calcutta Cricket Club in 2017. And to no surprise, his menu quickly garnered local and national attention—and a loyal following to boot.

Calcutta Cricket Club has been pushing the envelope on Calgary's dining scene with its soulful and authentic renderings of regional Indian cuisine in an equally lush and stylish dining room.

Named after the Calcutta Cricket & Football Club, founded in 1792 in what is now Kolkata, India, this oasis located on 17th Avenue sw is the brainchild of partners Cody Willis, Shovik Sengupta, Amber Anderson and Maya Gohill. The main dining room is a remarkable sight: bamboo bar stools, plush powder pink chairs, beautiful tile accents and palm-tree wallpaper that transport you to Kolkata. The look is distinctively stylish and the type of place you might take out-of-town guests to impress them.

Ginger-garlic paste

1 (2-inch) knob ginger, peeled
½ large head garlic,
  separated and peeled

Lamb shank kosha mangsho

1 large onion, coarsely chopped
6 Tbsp Ginger-Garlic Paste
  (see here, divided)
¼ cup plain Greek yogurt
4 lamb shanks
¼ cup mustard oil
4 whole cloves
4 green cardamom pods, cracked
  with a mortar and pestle
2 bay leaves
1 (1-inch) piece cinnamon stick

2 cups chopped tomatoes
1 Tbsp brown sugar
1 Tbsp ground coriander
1 Tbsp ground cumin
1 tsp ground turmeric
1 tsp red chili flakes
20 mint leaves, thinly sliced, for
  garnish
1 Tbsp dried rose petals, for garnish
Mishti Pulao (p. 47), roti or paratha
  to serve

Lamb Shank Kosha Mangsho

Serves 4

Lamb shanks should be part of every home cook's repertoire, and this traditional Bengali mutton curry is a good place to start. Give yourself plenty of time, because the shanks taste best when left to marinate in the refrigerator overnight, and if you are using whole spices, first toast and then grind them. The result is aromatic, tender to the bone and richly satisfying. Mustard oil can be found at The Cookbook Co. Cooks (p. 62) and Indian food stores.

Ginger-garlic paste Aim for equal amounts of garlic and ginger. In a blender, combine ginger and garlic and purée until smooth. Makes 6 tablespoons.

Lamb shank kosha mangsho Purée onion in a blender until smooth. (It should yield 2 cups.) Reserve half for the kosha braise.

In a large bowl, combine ¼ cup onion paste, 2 tablespoons ginger-garlic paste and yogurt. Add lamb shanks and mix to coat well. Cover, then refrigerate overnight.

Preheat oven to 300°F.

Heat mustard oil in a large ovenproof pan over medium heat. Add cloves, cardamom, bay leaves and cinnamon and fry for a few seconds, until fragrant. Add the remaining 1¾ cups onion paste and 4 tablespoons ginger-garlic paste and cook over medium-high heat until dark brown. Stir in tomatoes, sugar, coriander, cumin, turmeric, chili flakes and enough water to cover the shanks halfway. Cover and roast for 3 hours, or until the meat is falling off the bone and the water has evaporated. It should be deep and rich in colour.

Transfer shanks to a large serving platter and spoon sauce overtop. Garnish with mint and rose petals and serve with mishti pulao, roti or paratha.

Pictured | p. 46

Aromatic water

2 Tbsp granulated sugar

1 tsp rosewater

1 tsp kewra water

1 tsp kosher salt

1 tsp ghee

Mishti pulao

¼ cup mustard oil

¼ cup raw cashews

¼ cup raisins

5 whole cloves

3 green cardamom pods

1 bay leaf

1 (1-inch) piece cinnamon stick

1 cup basmati rice, rinsed and soaked for 30 minutes

2 Tbsp granulated sugar

1 tsp garam masala

1 tsp ground turmeric

1 tsp ground mace

2 cups Aromatic Water (see here)

1 Tbsp slivered almonds or pistachios, for garnish (optional)

Serves 4

Mishti Pulao

This popular Bengali rice dish is prepared with aromatic rosewater and kewra, an extract from the pandanus flower. Both are key South Asian ingredients and can be found in any Indian food store. Mustard oil can be found at The Cookbook Co. Cooks (p. 62) and Indian food stores.

Aromatic water In a medium saucepan, bring 2 cups water to a boil. Add all the ingredients, stir and remove from heat. Set aside until needed.

Mishti pulao Heat oil in a medium saucepan over medium heat. Add cashews and raisins and sauté for 5 minutes, or until golden brown. Add cloves, cardamom, bay leaf and cinnamon and fry for a few seconds, until fragrant.

Drain rice and add to pan. Stir in sugar, garam masala, turmeric and mace and pour in hot aromatic water. Increase heat to high and cook, uncovered, for 10 minutes. Do not stir (you don't want to break the grains). Remove from heat, cover and set aside for 10 minutes to steam.

Place on a large serving dish and fluff gently with a fork. Garnish with slivered almonds or pistachios, if using. Makes 4 cups.

Cassis Bistro

Gilles Brassart and Dominique Moussu

Chefs Gilles Brassart and Dominique Moussu opened Cassis Bistro in 2011 as an homage to the charming yet casual restaurants of the south of France. Serving up authentic flavours—we're talking *bouchées* (bites) of cod brandade, Alberta beef tartare with duck-fat potato chips, and a succulent duck breast with herb ricotta gnocchi, asparagus, wild mushrooms and honey truffle jus, a luxurious dish so filling that you think you won't have room left for dessert. (Yet we always do.)

Even the simplest dishes are worthy of a mention. Classics such as steak frites and quiche do not disappoint, and the lunch menu offers the entire *croque* family: croque madame, croque monsieur and croque mademoiselle.

The source of inspiration? Brassart was born and raised near Aix-en-Provence (home to Cézanne), in the south of France, surrounded by simple, fresh ingredients. "I spent a lot of my childhood in the kitchen with my mom and grandmother," he explains. "Where I'm from, the kitchen is the base and the heart of every family."

After two successful restaurant projects in San Francisco, Brassart moved to Calgary in 2008. "I wanted to share my culture with my guests and my community, because we believe that the most meaningful conversations happen at the table. So naturally, that table must always include good food and good wine."

ABOUT THE CHEF

Executive chef and partner Dominique Moussu brings the flavours of his diverse experiences to Cassis. Immediately after graduating from culinary school, he cooked at the gorgeous, historic Château de Locguénolé in Kervignac, Brittany, and at The Savoy in London, England. And as luck (for us) would have it, Moussu moved to Calgary and eventually became the executive chef for the Teatro Group.

Today, he is the operating partner of Cassis Bistro, Le Petit Boeuf Steak House and Suzette Brittany Bistro.

8 Alberta prime or high-quality
   beef cheeks
2 carrots, peeled and chopped
2 stalks celery, chopped
2 onions, chopped
4 shallots, chopped
1 bay leaf
4 whole cloves
2 (750-mL) bottles dry red wine, such
   as French Pinot Noir or Gamay

1 tsp kosher salt
Freshly ground black pepper, to taste
¾ cup + 1 Tbsp (1¾ sticks) unsalted
   butter
½ cup all-purpose flour
2 Tbsp oil for frying (canola,
   grapeseed, sunflower)
Mashed potatoes, to serve
Vegetable fricassee, to serve

Alberta Beef Cheeks Bourguignon

Serves 8

Beef cheeks have a rich, deep flavour and, when slow-cooked, become melt-in-the-mouth tender. It's no wonder chefs love cooking with them. If you cannot find beef cheeks, substitute any stew cut of beef: blade steak, chuck steak, shanks or oxtail. The beef cheeks need to marinate overnight for at least 12 hours, so be prepared to start the recipe a day in advance.

In a large bowl, combine beef cheeks, carrots, celery, onions, shallots, bay leaf, cloves and wine. Cover tightly with plastic wrap and refrigerate for 12 hours or overnight. Remove the beef cheeks from the marinade, pat them dry with paper towel and season with salt and pepper. Reserve the vegetable-wine marinade.

Preheat oven to 250°F.

Melt butter in a large Dutch oven over medium-high heat. Stir in flour and cook for 1 to 2 minutes, until the roux turns caramel coloured. Slowly whisk in vegetable-wine marinade, bring to a boil and reduce heat to medium. Simmer for 5 minutes, whisking continuously until smooth and thick. Reduce heat to medium-low, cover and keep warm.

Heat oil in a large frying pan over high heat. Add cheeks in batches, searing for 8 to 10 minutes on each side, until browned. Transfer cheeks to the Dutch oven, cover with an ovenproof lid or piece of aluminum foil and braise in the oven for 4 to 5 hours, until cheeks are fork tender.

Serve family-style with mashed potatoes and vegetable fricassee.

3 Tbsp olive oil
3 large yellow onions, thinly sliced
1 sheet puff pastry
12 white anchovies
1 roasted red pepper, thinly sliced
3 cups baby arugula
12 Niçoise olives, pitted

Pissaladière

Serves 4

Whether it's a snack with a bottle of rosé or a savoury starter for your next dinner party, this classic anchovy, caramelized onion and olive tart, hailing from southern France, is perfect for sharing. Anchovies add a hit of umami, but we prefer the milder white anchovy that is packed in vinegar and oil.

Heat oil in a heavy-bottomed saucepan over medium heat. Add onions and sauté for 10 minutes, or until onions start to soften and colour. Be sure to scrape the bottom of the pan so the onions don't stick. Increase heat to medium-high and sauté for another 10 to 15 minutes, until onions turn a rich, dark amber colour.

Preheat oven to 375°F. Line a baking sheet with parchment paper.

Roll out the pastry sheet to a ⅛-inch thickness. Transfer to the prepared baking sheet and, using a fork, puncture pastry to allow the steam to escape. Bake for 15 minutes, or until just slightly brown. Remove from oven, cool for 5 minutes and top with caramelized onions. Bake for another 20 minutes, or until golden brown. Remove from oven and set aside for 10 minutes to cool.

Place on a family-sized platter and arrange anchovies and roasted pepper on top in a diagonal pattern. Top with arugula and olives.

Cibo
Glen Manzer

boar bacon and fennel. For those whose carb of choice is pasta, orecchiette with sausage, peppers and olives, and penne with cherry tomatoes, ricotta, eggplant and mint are hearty homestyle dishes designed for comfort (and sharing if you're feeling generous).

Both locations have plenty of indoor seating, as well as popular patios, and can be booked for private events, including weddings. It's the type of environment designed for relaxation and for enjoying a delicious meal.

ABOUT THE CHEF

When he started cooking 30 years ago, Glen Manzer was on the vanguard of the sustainable and local food movement that forged relationships with area farmers and pushed for regional suppliers. Today, as executive chef and partner with Creative Restaurants Group, he oversees operations and builds the menus. In 2005, Manzer collaborated with The Cookbook Co. Cooks (p. 62) and chef friends to create a culinary fundraising event for the Alberta Cancer Foundation. It has since become an annual event that has raised over $120,000 to date. The Creative Restaurants Group also works with Restaurants for Change to improve and bolster community food programs. A strong advocate for the family dinner, Manzer also teaches and coaches the next generation of chefs.

Cibo is the delightful term used to describe a person who enjoys simple food in an unpretentious setting. Whether at its 17th Avenue sw location or its newest outpost on Centre Street, the restaurant serves classic and contemporary family-style Italian cuisine in an airy, vibrant and fun space.

Cibo is filled with cozy yet modern design features: refurbished brick and wood walls, old beams and hardwood floors. And it's a happening place: there's plenty of bustle and chatter among the crowds, though the overall atmosphere is decidedly relaxed and casual.

But let's talk food. Savoury aromas waft from the kitchen and speak of killer rustic Italian fare, which includes reliable share plates such as white bean hummus, and pizza with wild

1 lb chicken livers

2 to 3 cups whole milk

1 Tbsp kosher salt, plus extra to taste

1 Tbsp freshly ground black pepper

3 Tbsp + ¼ cup extra-virgin olive oil (divided), plus extra if needed

1 cup diced wild boar or good-quality bacon

1 small onion, finely chopped

4 cloves garlic, finely chopped

3 sprigs thyme, plus extra for garnish

¼ cup brandy

3 Tbsp capers, rinsed

3 Tbsp chopped Italian parsley

Grated zest and juice of 1 lemon, plus extra to taste

Cranberry mostarda, for garnish

Pickled shallot, for garnish

Olives, for garnish

Grissini (p. 55), crackers or fresh baguette, to serve

NOTE: The pâté can be wrapped in plastic wrap and stored in the freezer for up to 6 months. Thaw in the refrigerator for 12 hours before serving.

Serves 4

Chicken Liver Pâté

Whoever said "What am I, chopped liver?" has never tried *this* recipe. Here, the often overlooked side dish has its turn in the spotlight. With flavours and textures this distinct, who needs foie gras? If you can't find wild boar bacon, just use a good-quality bacon.

Put chicken livers in a bowl and add enough milk to cover. Set aside and soak for 2 hours. Drain and reserve chicken liver. Discard milk.

Using a paring knife, remove any blemishes or connective veins from livers and pat dry with paper towel. Place on a baking sheet and season generously with salt and pepper.

Heat 3 tablespoons olive oil in a frying pan over medium heat. Carefully add livers, working in batches, if necessary, to avoid overcrowding and sauté for 2 minutes on each side, or until centres are slightly pink. (Do not overcook or livers will become tough.) Add a splash more oil if needed. Transfer livers to a plate and set aside.

Heat a splash of oil in the same pan set over medium-high heat, then add wild boar (or bacon) and cook for 5 to 10 minutes, until slightly crispy. Add onion, garlic and thyme and sauté for 10 minutes, or until thoroughly cooked but not browned. Remove pan from heat and add brandy. Return pan to heat and bring to a simmer, scraping the bottom of the pan to release any browned bits. Cook for another minute to reduce the liquid. Return reserved livers and their resting juices to the pan, reduce heat to medium-low and cook slightly. Remove thyme stems. Set aside to cool slightly.

In a food processor, purée capers, parsley and lemon zest and juice. With the motor still running, slowly add ¼ cup oil to form a thick paste. Add more oil, if necessary, to achieve the desired consistency. Add half of the liver mixture and process until smooth. Transfer liver paste to a bowl.

Place the other half of the mixture on a large cutting board and finely chop. Add to the bowl of liver paste and mix well. (Alternatively, process everything in a food processor for a smoother texture.) Season with salt and lemon. Set aside to cool.

Transfer pâté to a serving bowl or large ramekins. Garnish with thyme, cranberry mostarda, pickled shallots and olives.

Serve with grissini, crackers or baguette.

Pictured | p. 54

½ tsp granulated sugar

1½ cups lukewarm (105°F to 110°F) water

1 Tbsp instant yeast

2 to 4 Tbsp extra-virgin olive oil, plus extra for greasing

4 cups all-purpose flour, plus extra for dusting

2 tsp kosher salt, plus extra to taste

Freshly ground black pepper, to taste

Chicken Liver Pâté (p. 53) or your favourite dip, to serve

Grissini

Serves 15

Grissini—slender, crunchy, dip-able Italian breadsticks—look elegant as an edible centrepiece for assorted dips and are truly the best finger food. You'll wonder why you haven't made these before. The dough can be kept in an airtight container at room temperature and made up to 5 days in advance. This very forgiving dough can be twisted, knotted or flattened.

In the bowl of a stand mixer fitted with the hook attachment, stir sugar and lukewarm water until the sugar is dissolved. Stir in yeast and add 2 tablespoons oil (if mixing by hand, add 4 tablespoons instead), flour and salt. Mix until dough is smooth and elastic. If the mixture is sticky, add a bit more flour.

Oil a large bowl. Transfer dough to the bowl, cover with plastic wrap and set aside at room temperature to proof for 90 minutes or until doubled in size.

Preheat oven to 350°F. Line one or two baking sheets with parchment paper and lightly grease.

Transfer dough to a lightly floured work surface and roll into an 8- × 15-inch rectangle, ⅛ inch thick. Using a pasta cutter, cut into ½-inch strips. (If you want longer grissini, cut them lengthwise. For shorter sticks, cut widthwise.) Gently place strips on the prepared baking sheet, evenly spacing them ½ inch apart.

Brush grissini with oil and season with salt and pepper. If desired, gently twist for a decorative look. Bake for 10 to 15 minutes, until crispy and golden. Remove from oven and set aside onto a wire rack to cool.

Stand grissini up in an attractive container and serve with chicken liver pâté or dip.

Cilantro
Lancelot Monteiro

slow-braised short ribs on p. 58 are melt-in-your-mouth tender.)

On sunny days, patrons covet the seating in the secluded courtyard, where Virginia creepers climb the walls and leafy, fairy light–festooned trees provide canopy. When the experience makes one feel like they're miles away from the hustle and bustle of Calgary, does one really need more convincing?

ABOUT THE CHEF

Chef Lancelot Monteiro is a born-and-bred Calgarian. His passion for food and cooking prompted him to leave Mount Royal University, where he was pursuing an aviation certificate. Having apprenticed under Chef Kevin Turner at Calgary's highly acclaimed Brava Bistro, Monteiro graduated from SAIT's (Southern Alberta Institute of Technology's) culinary program with honours in 2007. He then travelled to France, Italy, Spain and, in the United States, Hawaii, to expand and hone his craft and to master a variety of flavours. In 2010, he returned to Calgary to join Canadian Rocky Mountain Resorts, working under long-time Cilantro head Chef Ken Canavan. "I'm constantly inspired to create and perfect dishes for Cilantro's guests," says Monteiro, "but admittedly, I love cooking for my two biggest fans—my kids."

This elegant downtown restaurant is all about the simple pleasures, with a pared-back style, friendly staff, and tasty small and large plates made for sharing.

Cilantro was the first restaurant in Alberta to import and use an Italian wood-burning pizza oven. And since 1988, that very oven, nested at the back of the upstairs dining room, has been responsible for churning out perfectly blistered, California-style thin-crust pizza.

A menu chock full of regional provisions and house-made elements (preserves, pickles and pastas) add to the charm. Few things are more Canadian than bison and elk, and the menu features both from Canadian Rocky Mountain Ranch's game farm. (The bison

▶ Braised Bison Short Ribs, Parsnip Purée, Cola Braise | p. 58

Bison short ribs

2½ lbs bison short ribs

Kosher salt, plus extra to taste

3 cups veal or beef stock

2 cups canned stewed tomatoes

3 Tbsp canola or olive oil (divided)

3 stalks celery, coarsely chopped

2 carrots, coarsely chopped

1 onion, coarsely chopped

5 cloves garlic, crushed

2 bay leaves

5 sprigs thyme

3 sprigs rosemary

1 cup dry red wine

1 (355-mL) can of your favourite cola

2 cups micro arugula, for garnish

Freshly ground black pepper, to taste

Braised Bison Short Ribs, Parsnip Purée, Cola Braise

Serves 4 to 6

Cilantro's signature bison ribs are perfect year-round. The grass-fed bison are raised without the use of hormones or antibiotics at Canadian Rocky Mountain Ranch, owned and operated by Canadian Rocky Mountain Resorts (Cilantro's parent company). The high-quality game meats can be found at Urban Butcher locations in Mission and Willow Park. This versatile recipe can also be prepared with elk or beef ribs.

Bison short ribs Generously salt the rib racks, wrap in plastic wrap and refrigerate overnight.

In a large saucepan, combine stock and tomatoes and bring to a boil.

Cut ribs down to 4 bones per rack. Heat 1 tablespoon oil in a large cast-iron pan over high heat. Working in batches to avoid over-crowding, add ribs and sear for 3 to 5 minutes on each side, until a crust forms. Transfer ribs to a plate and set aside. Repeat with the remaining batches.

Preheat oven to 300°F.

Heat the remaining 2 tablespoons oil in a Dutch oven over medium-high heat. Add celery, carrots and onion and sauté for 10 minutes, or until softened and slightly browned. Add garlic, bay leaves and herbs, then pour in wine and cola and deglaze the pan. Add ribs and stock mixture to the pot and bring to a boil.

Top with a parchment-paper lid (cut out a piece of parchment the same size as the pot) and cook in the oven for 4 hours 20 minutes, or until meat is tender. Do not use the pot lid to cover it (the parchment protects the surface of the dish from drying out too much but still allows the sauce to reduce). Check the oven temperature every hour to ensure that the mixture is at a slow simmer and not a full boil. Remove from oven and set aside for 30 minutes.

Parsnip purée

2 Tbsp canola oil

4 to 6 parsnips, peeled and chopped

1 stalk celery, chopped

1 leek, white part only, chopped

½ onion, chopped

2 large cloves garlic, crushed

1 bay leaf

4 sprigs thyme

1 sprig rosemary

⅓ cup dry white wine

2 cups chicken stock, plus extra if needed

1 cup whipping cream, plus extra if needed

1 Tbsp kosher salt

2 tsp ground white pepper

Parsnip purée Heat oil in a saucepan over medium-low heat. Add parsnips, celery, leek and onion and sauté for 10 to 15 minutes, until softened. Add garlic, bay leaf and herbs and cook for 5 minutes. Pour in wine and cook for 10 minutes, or until liquid is reduced by half. Add stock, cream, salt and pepper and bring to a boil. Cover, reduce heat to low and simmer for 30 to 35 minutes, until parsnips are tender to the touch. Discard thyme, rosemary and bay leaf.

Transfer mixture to a blender and purée until smooth. If necessary, add more cream or stock to achieve your desired consistency. Keep warm and set aside.

Assembly Using a slotted spoon, transfer meat to a plate. Skim the fat off the surface of the braising liquid and discard. Bring liquid to a boil over medium-high heat and boil for 20 to 30 minutes, or until reduced by half. Strain.

Return sauce to saucepan, add meat and gently heat through over medium-low heat.

Place a generous spoonful of parsnip purée in the centre of each plate and carefully place bison ribs on top. Drizzle sauce overtop and finish with micro arugula. Season with salt and pepper to taste.

Pictured | p. 57

Pickled cucumber salad
¼ cup rice vinegar
1 Tbsp granulated sugar
1 tsp ground white pepper
1 Tbsp kosher salt
Generous pinch of fresh dill
1 large English cucumber,
   thinly sliced into discs
1 shallot, thinly sliced

Whiskey barbecue sauce
⅓ cup vegetable oil
1 small onion, coarsely chopped
6 cloves garlic
1 stalk celery, finely chopped
1 small knob ginger, peeled and
   finely chopped
1 Tbsp smoked paprika
1½ tsp cayenne pepper
¼ cup whiskey
1 cup tomato paste
⅔ cup packed brown sugar
1 cup apple cider vinegar
¼ cup blackstrap molasses
1 Tbsp kosher salt
1 Tbsp freshly ground black pepper

Barbecue elk ribs
½ cup packed brown sugar
1 Tbsp dry mustard
1 Tbsp dried oregano
1 Tbsp smoked paprika
1 Tbsp garlic powder
1 Tbsp onion powder
1 Tbsp kosher salt
1 Tbsp freshly ground black pepper
1½ tsp cayenne pepper
2½ to 3 lbs elk side ribs
4 cups chicken stock
2 yellow onions, thinly sliced
1 cup Whiskey Barbecue Sauce
   (see here)

Whiskey-Glazed Elk Ribs with Pickled Cucumber Salad

Serves 4 to 6

Sticky, sweet ribs with a subtle whiskey kick are paired with a refreshing cucumber salad for a signature summer dish. Use your favourite whiskey and invest in a good-quality molasses to bring the barbecue sauce to life. Elk side ribs are available at Urban Butcher.

Pickled cucumber salad In a large jar with a lid, combine vinegar, sugar, pepper, salt and dill and seal the jar. Shake well until the sugar and salt dissolve. Add cucumbers and shallot. Refrigerate for up to 5 days.

Whiskey barbecue sauce Heat oil in a frying pan over medium-high heat. Add onion, garlic, celery and ginger and sauté for 5 to 10 minutes, until onion is soft and translucent. Reduce heat to low and sauté for another 15 to 20 minutes, until onions are thoroughly cooked and sweet but not caramelized. Add paprika and cayenne pepper and cook for 2 to 3 minutes.

Pour in whiskey and deglaze the pan. Pour in 1 cup water, stir in tomato paste and bring mixture to a boil. Add sugar, vinegar, molasses, salt and pepper. Reduce heat to low and simmer for 2 to 3 hours.

Using an immersion blender, blend the mixture until smooth, then set aside to cool.

Barbecue elk ribs In a large bowl, combine sugar, mustard, oregano, paprika, garlic powder, onion powder, salt, pepper and cayenne pepper.

Pat ribs dry with paper towel. Add ribs to bowl, rub in marinade and refrigerate overnight.

Preheat oven to 300°F.

Put ribs in a large, deep baking dish such as a turkey roaster. Pour in stock, add onions and cover with aluminum foil. Bake for 4 to 6 hours, until meat recedes down the bone. Transfer ribs to a plate and let rest for 10 to 15 minutes.

Preheat a grill over medium-high heat. Pour half of the barbecue sauce into a bowl and brush it over ribs. Grill ribs for 3 to 5 minutes on each side, brushing on more sauce with each flip. Discard any sauce that's leftover in the bowl.

Remove ribs from the grill. Pour the remaining barbecue sauce into a clean bowl. Brush sauce on the ribs and let rest for 10 to 15 minutes.

Assembly Place ribs on a large platter and serve family-style with cucumber salad.

The Cookbook Co. Cooks

Melissa Kennedy and Sarah Boucher

Established in 1984, The Cookbook Co. Cooks began as a specialty bookstore, expanding over the years to include all things culinary. Located in what was once an old railway warehouse, the charming 11th Avenue store—still with the original interior detail, such as hardwood floors, huge support beams and exposed brick—is Calgary's premier destination for current and classic cookbooks, specialty foods and kitchenware.

It also offers a range of cooking classes for both beginner and seasoned cooks. In these informal yet informative classes, you can master basic knife skills, prepare paella or discover national cuisines, including Vietnamese, Thai and Portuguese. The Cookbook Co. Cooks remains one of the best gathering places in the city for people who love to cook and eat good food.

ABOUT THE CHEFS

Since 2012, Chef Melissa Kennedy has worked at The Cookbook Co. Cooks as its catering and pantry chef, as well as a culinary instructor. Originally from Brantford, Ontario, Kennedy thanks her father for his early influence on her decision to become a chef. Soon after graduating from Fanshawe College's culinary arts program, Kennedy headed to Tuscany, where she perfected her pasta-making technique and worked with world-renowned butcher Dario Cecchini. Kennedy is happy to now be part of Calgary's flourishing food scene, and to put her personal twists on classic dishes.

Sarah Boucher joined The Cookbook Co. Cooks team in 2017 as the assistant store manager and culinary instructor. She is most at home when her hands are in the dirt. "When I was little, we used to help prepare vegetables on my grandparents' farm," Boucher says. "Both of my parents love to cook, but my grandmother

Nannie was a notable influence on me. She was always canning or baking fresh rolls or pies."

Boucher's long-term goal is to cook with everything she grows and raises. A graduate of SAIT's (Southern Alberta Institute of Technology's) culinary program, she has worked in top restaurants, including Anju, The Coup and Briggs Kitchen + Bar. She is committed to supporting ethical and sustainable producers, and volunteers at Blue Mountain Biodynamic Farms.

Falafel

¾ cup dried chickpeas
⅓ cup dried red lentils
½ yellow onion
2 cloves garlic
1 fresh jalapeño pepper
1 bunch cilantro
½ bunch Italian parsley
1 tsp cumin seeds
1 tsp coriander seeds

1 tsp green cardamom pods
¼ heaping cup chickpea flour, plus extra if needed
1½ tsp baking powder
2 tsp kosher salt
Canola, grapeseed or peanut oil, for frying
Pita bread, to serve (optional)
Pickles, sliced tomatoes and onions, to serve (optional)

Yogurt dip

½ cup Greek yogurt
Freshly ground black pepper, to taste
1 clove garlic, finely chopped
Grated zest and juice of ½ lemon
Kosher salt, to taste

Serves 8 to 10

Falafel with Yogurt Dip

These fluffy and flavourful falafel will change your life. Well, that may be a tad of an overstatement, but serve them with a creamy yogurt dip and you will be inspired to eat these at every chance you get. This version is the happy result of a pot of over-cooked red lentils. The trick to light, fluffy falafel is to add as little chickpea flour as possible—use just enough to bring the mixture together. Falafel freeze well and can be warmed up for a quick appetizer. The chickpeas will need to soak overnight first.

Falafel Soak chickpeas in a large bowl of water overnight.

In a saucepan, combine lentils and 3 cups water and bring to a boil. Reduce heat to medium-low and simmer for 20 minutes, or until lentils are very soft. Drain well and set aside to cool.

Drain and rinse chickpeas under cold running water. Put soaked chickpeas in a food processor and purée until there are no large pieces but before the mixture turns into a coarse paste. Transfer puréed chickpeas to a large bowl and set aside.

Add lentils to the food processor and purée to a paste. Add lentil paste to the bowl of puréed chickpeas and mix.

Whirl onion, garlic and jalapeño in the food processor until finely chopped. Add cilantro and parsley and whirl for another minute. Add onion mixture to chickpea-lentil paste and, using your hands, mix until ingredients are well combined and evenly distributed.

Toast cumin, coriander and cardamom in a dry frying pan over medium-high heat for 4 minutes, or until fragrant. Remove from heat, cool and grind to a fine powder. Set aside.

In a small bowl, combine chickpea flour, baking powder and toasted ground spices. Season with salt. Sprinkle this mixture over the chickpea mixture and, using your hands, squeeze the mixture between your fingers to incorporate the dry ingredients. The mixture should be slightly wet and hold its shape when squeezed together. (If the mixture is too wet, add a little more chickpea flour. Take care to not add too much or falafel will have a heavy texture.)

Preheat oven to 200°F. Line a baking sheet with parchment paper.

Form mixture into 2-inch-diameter patties and place on the prepared baking sheet. Heat ¼ inch of oil in a large heavy-bottomed frying pan over high heat. Carefully lower falafel into the pan, working in batches to avoid overcrowding. Fry for 2 minutes per side, or until golden and a crust has formed. Transfer to a baking sheet lined with paper towel, then keep warm in the oven. Repeat with remaining falafel.

Yogurt dip In a small bowl, combine all ingredients except salt. Season with salt.

Assembly Place falafel on a serving platter and place generous dollops of dip overtop. Serve with pita bread, pickles, sliced tomatoes and onions, if using.

Preserved lemon–thyme butter

1 cup (2 sticks) unsalted butter, room temperature

2 Tbsp finely chopped preserved lemon

Grated zest of 2 lemons

2 tsp chopped thyme

1 tsp kosher salt

Ricotta

4 cups organic whole milk

2 cups organic buttermilk

1 tsp kosher salt

3 Tbsp freshly squeezed lemon juice or apple cider vinegar

Pasta

2 cups all-purpose flour, plus extra for dusting

3 medium eggs

1 tsp kosher salt

Pasta filling

1½ cups fresh ricotta (see here)

¼ cup grated hard cheese (preferably Grizzly Gouda from Sylvan Star Cheese)

1 tsp kosher salt, plus extra to taste

Freshly ground black pepper, to taste

Assembly

½ cup Preserved Lemon–Thyme Butter (see here)

Shavings of pecorino, for garnish

Maldon salt, for garnish

Finely chopped chives, for garnish

Ricotta-Stuffed Pasta with a Preserved Lemon–Thyme Butter Sauce

Serves 6 (Makes 36 stuffed pasta)

Homemade ricotta is a revelation, and its superior texture and taste prove that good things do come to those who take the time. It is fun to make (honestly!) but in a pinch, store-bought ricotta or a creamy chèvre will do nicely. The preserved lemon–thyme butter is a delicious taste-booster to have in your pantry. We recommend making extra for topping steak right off the grill, stuffing under the skin of roasting chicken or adding to the centre of a burger—the possibilities are endless.

Preserved lemon–thyme butter In a stand mixer fitted with the paddle attachment, mix the ingredients well to combine. Set aside. (Makes 1 cup.)

Leftover butter can be stored in a glass jar for up to 3 weeks.

Ricotta In a large heavy-bottomed saucepan, combine milk, buttermilk and salt over medium heat. Gently stir the mixture, then leave untouched until it begins to steam and reaches a temperature of 160°F.

Add lemon juice or vinegar and very gently pull a wooden spoon through the mixture to distribute the lemon. Continue to heat until curds start to form and the temperature reaches 185°F, about 10 minutes. Do not allow the mixture to boil. Turn off the heat and set aside, untouched, to cool and curdle. Once cool, cover and refrigerate overnight. Refrigerating isn't mandatory, but it creates a creamier ricotta.

Line a sieve with cheesecloth and place over a bowl. Gently spoon the mixture into the sieve and drain for 2 hours, or until very thick and creamy. Thin it out with more cream or whey if necessary. This should yield 1½ cups ricotta. (You can reserve the whey to add to soups, stews or baking recipes that call for water. If you don't use it within 2 days, freeze or discard.) *continued overleaf...*

Pasta Put flour in a bowl and make a well in the centre. Add eggs and salt and, using your hands, mix the ingredients until a shaggy dough is formed. Turn out onto a lightly floured work surface and knead until it forms one smooth and very firm dough. If necessary, add more flour to the work surface to prevent the dough from sticking. Cover with a dish towel and let rest for at least 30 minutes or overnight. This allows the gluten to relax and makes for easier rolling.

Cut the dough into 4 pieces. Take 1 piece to work with, covering the rest with a dish towel to prevent them from drying out.

Set your pasta roller to its thickest setting. Sprinkle a piece of dough with flour, then pinch one edge and flatten it enough to fit into the machine. Roll the dough through.

Lay the long side of the dough toward you and fold it into thirds, like you would a business letter. Turn and pinch the short edge, feed it through the rollers and roll the dough through the machine. Repeat this folding and rolling step three more times at this setting. Set the roller one thinner and roll the dough through again. Repeat until you reach the penultimate setting. Feed the pasta through the roller once or twice. The pasta should be thin, smooth and almost translucent.

Lay sheets out on the work surface and, using a 3-inch round cookie cutter (or a glass), cut dough into rounds. Lay them on a lightly floured dish towel and cover with another dish towel to prevent them from drying out. Cut at least 36 pieces. (You can make more and freeze the stuffed pasta, or save any leftover pasta to make lasagna noodles.) Set aside.

Pasta filling In a large bowl, thoroughly combine all ingredients. Adjust seasoning to taste.

Assembly Lightly dust a baking sheet with flour and set aside.

Place a generous teaspoon of filling in the centre of each pasta round. Using a pastry brush or your finger, dampen the edges with water. Fold over the dough to form a half-moon, then press tightly to seal. Dust with flour, then place on the prepared baking sheet. Cover with a dish towel. Repeat with the remaining pasta rounds and filling. (At this stage, if you like, the stuffed pasta can be placed in the freezer for future use—see Note.)

Bring a large saucepan of salted water to a boil. Working in batches, carefully lower the stuffed pasta into the water and gently stir to prevent the pieces from sticking together.

Cook for 4 minutes, or until they float to the surface. Cook for another minute. Transfer the cooked pasta to a platter and repeat with the remaining pasta.

Melt preserved lemon–thyme butter in a small frying pan over medium heat, adjusting the heat as necessary to prevent the lemon from scorching. Drizzle butter over pasta, then garnish with pecorino, salt and chives. Serve family-style.

The Coup
Dalia Kohen

and community sets them apart: they use only recyclable paper products and run on 100% wind-power "off-set" (since they are not able to put a windmill on the roof, or access the power downtown, they pay 100% of their bill to Bullfrog Power, to build more windmills and allow for new neighbourhoods in Calgary to access the power generated). They use compost for the restaurant garden, plant 36 trees each month through Tree Canada and provide food to the Leftovers Foundation to reduce waste. This is all to offer a food quality that they can stand behind. Suffice to say, The Coup's ever-evolving menu continues to make for exceptional plant-based dining.

ABOUT THE CHEF

Dalia Kohen attended Natural Gourmet Institute in New York City, where the focus is on nutritious cooking with local, whole and organic foods. From there, she worked at the venerable kitchens of ABC Kitchen and the now-defunct Annisa. This incredible experience greatly influenced and enhanced The Coup's kitchen, bringing a wide range of nut cheeses, ferments and dehydrated items (such as watermelon prosciutto) to the menu.

Kohen continues to draw as much inspiration from home-grown ingredients as she does from her travels, creating a cuisine that embraces big, bold flavours from cultures around the world. And much to our delight, Calgarians support Kohen's ever-expanding vision of inspired plant-based meals.

The Coup is arguably one of the most modern and exciting destinations to come out of Calgary. Since 2004, they've been serving up delicious globally-minded vegan and vegetarian food dishes: The Green House Effect is a bowl of chickpeas, feta, olives, sunflower sprouts and summer radish crammed full of rainbow goodness while a Giant Panda sees seitan served with yellow curry peanut sauce, pandan rice and a zesty Thai citrus salad. In addition to the covetable vegetarian dishes, The Coup creates some of the freshest and most intriguing cocktails in town.

This ethical vegetarian restaurant is the first of its kind in Calgary. Sure, the ingredients are organic and local. Sure, everything is made from scratch. Sure, they've also committed to rennet-free cheese and GMO-free soy products. But their responsibility to the environment

Spring radish soup

3 Tbsp grapeseed oil

6 small stalks celery, coarsely chopped

3 carrots, coarsely chopped

1 onion, coarsely chopped

2½ tsp kosher salt (divided), plus extra to taste

1 leek, white part only, sliced

1 small zucchini, peeled and coarsely chopped

¼ cup white wine

5 cloves garlic

½ cup olive oil

2 cups red spring radishes, ends trimmed and quartered

2 Tbsp unsalted butter

2 small white potatoes

Juice of 1 lemon

Ground white pepper, to taste

Garnishes

Crème fraîche

Grated lemon zest

1 to 2 radishes, thinly sliced

Chives, finely chopped (optional)

Amaranth microgreens (optional)

Spring Radish Soup with Citrus Zest

Serves 4

This pretty blush-coloured soup is topped with crème fraîche and herbs, creating a heightened dish that is designed to both impress and satisfy. When cooked, radishes mellow out to a delicate flavour. We recommend you make your own stock in order to adjust the flavours to your preference, but a good-quality, store-bought vegetable stock is perfectly fine to use as well.

Spring radish soup Heat grapeseed oil in a medium saucepan over medium-high heat. Add celery, carrots, onion and 1½ teaspoons salt and sauté for 5 minutes, or until vegetables have slightly softened. Add leek and zucchini, reduce heat and sauté for 15 minutes, or until vegetables are softened but do not brown.

Pour in wine and deglaze the pan. Pour in 4 cups water and bring to a boil over high heat. Reduce heat to medium-low, cover and simmer the stock for 35 to 45 minutes.

Preheat oven to 400°F.

Place garlic in a small, ovenproof container and top with enough olive oil (about ½ cup) to fully cover them, so they don't burn. Roast for 30 minutes, or until garlic has a spreadable texture. (The resulting garlic oil can be used to enhance salad dressings.)

Line a baking sheet with parchment paper. Place radishes on the prepared baking sheet and dot them with butter. Roast for 20 to 25 minutes, tossing occasionally, until they can be easily pierced with a fork. Do not overcook—you want them to retain their bright pink colour.

Meanwhile, put potatoes and the remaining 1 teaspoon salt in a saucepan of water. Boil for 45 minutes, or until potatoes can be easily pierced by a fork. Drain and set aside to cool.

Strain stock into a bowl and discard vegetables. In a blender, combine radishes, pan drippings, potatoes, roasted garlic and 1 cup strained stock. Start on low, gradually increasing the speed. Blend until smooth, adding more stock as needed. If you prefer a thinner soup, add extra stock.

Add lemon juice (it will instantly turn the soup pink). Season with white pepper and more salt or lemon as desired.

Ladle soup into bowls and top with a dollop of crème fraîche, lemon zest, radishes, chives and amaranth microgreens, if using.

Celeriac cream

1 medium celeriac, peeled and cut into 1-inch pieces (about 2 cups)
2 stalks celery, coarsely chopped
2 Tbsp + 1 cup olive oil
1 tsp kosher salt, plus extra to taste
3 cloves garlic
1 shallot, peeled and halved
1 cup macadamia nuts, soaked for 2 hours in cold water
1 tsp freshly squeezed lemon juice
½ cup almond milk
¼ tsp ground white pepper
Celery leaves, for garnish

Dough

¼ cup spelt flour
2 cups unbleached all-purpose flour (divided), plus extra for dusting
1 Tbsp charcoal powder
½ tsp kosher salt

Wild mushroom filling

2 Tbsp unsalted butter (or Earth Balance Buttery Spread for vegans)
6 cups wild or assorted seasonal mushrooms, chopped
2 cloves garlic, finely chopped
½ tsp ground white pepper
¼ tsp kosher salt
2 Tbsp white wine

Makes 40 to 50 dumplings

Wild Mushroom Dumplings with Celeriac Cream

These crowd-pleasing dumplings require a bit of preparation time, but they're well worth the effort. (Plus, they're fun to prepare with others!) Charcoal powder, which can be found at most large supermarkets, is used as a vegetarian alternative to squid ink. However, if you do not want black dough, omit the charcoal and add an extra tablespoon flour.

Celeriac cream Preheat oven to 350°F. Line a baking sheet with parchment paper.

In a large bowl, combine celeriac and celery. Add 2 tablespoons olive oil and salt and toss to coat. Spread vegetables on the prepared baking sheet and bake for 45 minutes, or until they can be easily pierced with a fork.

Meanwhile, place garlic and shallot in a small ovenproof container and cover with the remaining 1 cup olive oil. Bake for 30 minutes, or until they have a spreadable texture. Transfer to a plate and set aside. Reserve oil.

Drain macadamia nuts, then put in a blender. Add celeriac mixture, roasted garlic and shallot, lemon juice, 1 tablespoon garlic-shallot oil and almond milk. Add water to achieve your desired consistency. Season with salt and white pepper.

Dough In a stand mixer fitted with the hook attachment, combine spelt flour and all but 1 tablespoon all-purpose flour, charcoal and salt. Mix on medium speed until incorporated.

With the motor still running, slowly pour in 1 cup just-boiled water and mix for 4 to 5 minutes, until dough is smooth and firm. Put dough in a plastic bag and set aside to rest for 2 hours. (Dough can also be refrigerated for up to 2 days. Let it stand for 1 hour at room temperature before using.)

Transfer dough to a lightly floured work surface and cut into 6 even pieces. Take 1 piece to work with, covering the rest with a lint-free dish towel to prevent them from drying out.

Roll dough into a small round ball, then press it down evenly onto your work surface with your palm. Using a rolling pin, roll from the centre outward to an even ⅛-inch thickness. Lightly dust both sides of the dough disk with flour and set under the dish towel until you are ready to add the filling. (Alternatively, use a pasta machine.) Repeat with remaining dough pieces.

Using a 3-inch round cutter or glass, cut out rounds from the dough disks. Excess dough can be rerolled and cut out. Makes 40 to 50.

Wild mushroom filling Melt butter in a medium frying pan over medium heat. Add mushrooms and sauté for 5 minutes, or until their water is released and reduced. Add garlic, pepper and salt. Reduce heat to medium-low and cook for another 2 to 3 minutes, until liquid has evaporated. Pour in wine and deglaze the pan. Set mushrooms aside to cool.

Dumpling Dust both sides of dough rounds with flour. Place 1 heaping teaspoon filling in the centre of each, taking care not to overfill. Fold the two sides up to meet in the centre and pinch together. Bring one of the open sides up to meet in the centre and pinch together to join up with the other fold. (It will look like a mermaid tail.) Fold the other open end to meet in the centre in the same way, and seal to the other seam. The dough should be sticky enough to seal without water. The dumpling should look like a four-cornered pillow.

Prepare a double boiler or bamboo steamer. Cut a piece of parchment paper to line the bottom of the boiler pan or steamer and place dumplings on top. Bring the water to a boil in the bottom pot, place top pan or steamer on top and cover. Steam dumplings for 7 to 9 minutes, until a toothpick can pierce the thickest fold without resistance.

Assembly Spoon 2 tablespoons celeriac cream into the centre of the plate and spread into a line slightly wider than the dumplings. Angle dumplings on top of the cream.

Drizzle with garlic-shallot oil (reserve the remaining garlic oil for another use) and garnish the plate with a small celery leaf. Serve immediately.

Cuisine et Château

Marnie Fudge and Thierry Meret

Cuisine et Château wants you to cook and have fun with it. Their guided all-inclusive, luxury culinary tours to France are designed for those who want to venture to hone their culinary skills, but the in-house program is just as interesting at its current state-of-the-art Interactive Culinary Centre. It offers not only a wide array of cooking classes but also custom corporate events and even after-school programs for children between the ages of 8 and 13. And for those looking to refine their wine palate, the interactive Wine Series reminds us that the best way to learn about wine is by drinking it.

It's an impressive list of courses. Whether you want to sharpen your knife skills or get a primer on cooking fish, Cuisine et Château ensures that everyone, regardless of skill level, will always learn something new about food and cooking. The cooking classes are kept small, the instructors—all professional chefs—imparting the knowledge and how-to that will inspire home cooks to host dinners with the confidence of a seasoned chef.

ABOUT THE CHEFS

Pastry chef Marnie Fudge has always been an innovator. In 1995, she launched Basil Ranch, one of the first businesses in the city to supply restaurants with fresh herbs. She later went on to found Palette Fine Foods, an award-winning gourmet food manufacturer. But her true calling as a pastry chef led her to baking at Calgary's Hotel Arts and teach at SAIT (Southern Alberta Institute of Technology).

Chef de cuisine Thierry Meret has worked as a chef throughout Europe as well as at Calgary's best restaurants and has taught at SAIT. His food is inspired by regional cooking techniques and local ingredients.

Cuisine et Château's program is led by exceptionally qualified instructors: all are professional chefs with international experience and dedicated to providing guests with unique culinary experiences.

Parmesan shortbread

½ cup (1 stick) unsalted butter, room temperature

⅓ cup finely grated Parmesan

1 clove garlic, finely chopped

1 tsp fennel seeds, crushed

1 tsp coarse salt, kosher salt or Maldon salt

Pinch of cayenne pepper

1½ cups all-purpose flour

Arugula-lemon dip

1 cup baby arugula

⅓ cup sour cream

¼ cup mascarpone

1 tsp finely chopped garlic

1 tsp grated lemon zest

2 tsp freshly squeezed lemon juice

Freshly ground black pepper, to taste

1 Tbsp toasted sunflower seeds

Parmesan Shortbread with Arugula-Lemon Dip

Makes 24

You'll wonder why you've never tried to make cheesy shortbread before, it's so easy and delicious. Paired with the rich shortbread, the arugula-lemon dip has a refreshing peppery edge.

Parmesan shortbread Preheat oven to 350°F. Line a baking sheet with parchment paper.

In a mixing bowl, beat butter for 30 seconds. Add Parmesan, garlic, fennel seeds, salt and cayenne and mix to combine. Add half the flour, mix to incorporate, add the remaining flour and mix until a smooth dough is formed.

Divide dough in two and roll each into a log, 2 inches in diameter. Wrap in plastic wrap and refrigerate for at least 15 minutes, or until chilled through. Remove from the refrigerator and unwrap. Slice into wheels ¼ inch thick and place on the prepared baking sheet.

Bake for 12 to 15 minutes, until slightly puffed and lightly browned. Remove from oven and set aside to cool.

Arugula-lemon dip Fill a large bowl with ice water. Set aside.

Bring a large pan of salted water to a boil. Add arugula and using a wooden spoon, press down to submerge and cook for 5 seconds. Drain, then transfer to the ice bath to cool completely. Drain and squeeze out excess water.

Roughly chop the arugula, then transfer it to a food processor. Add the remaining ingredients except sunflower seeds and purée until smooth.

To serve Scoop dip into a serving dish and garnish with sunflower seeds. Serve with Parmesan shortbread.

▶ Bouillabaisse | p. 80

Prawn stock

2 Tbsp olive oil

1 small onion, chopped

1 bay leaf

1 star anise

1 strip lemon zest

1 tsp kosher salt (or ¼ tsp fine sea salt)

1 tsp white peppercorns

½ tsp coriander seeds

½ tsp fennel seeds

1 cup prawn shells

2 Tbsp tomato paste

1 tomato, chopped

¼ cup white wine

3 cups cold fish stock or water

Bouillabaisse

3 cups hot Prawn Stock (see here)

1 cup vegetables such as carrot, leek, fennel, celery, celeriac, red onion and sweet pepper, cut into matchsticks

4 oz salmon fillet, cut into ¾-inch cubes

4 oz white fish such as halibut, cod or snapper, cut into ½-inch cubes

Kosher salt and freshly ground black pepper, to taste

6 (size 21/25) prawns, peeled and deveined

2 large scallops, halved

6 to 8 live mussels, scrubbed

Fire-roasted peppers

2 red bell peppers

Serves 2

Bouillabaisse

Cuisine et Château's take on the classic Provençal fish stew is delicious and satisfying. *Rouille* is a roasted red pepper dip that's traditionally spread on slices of baguette and placed on top of bouillabaisse, but in this version it's served in a small bowl alongside the baguette. It can be made in advance and reserved until you are ready to make the bouillabaisse.

Prawn stock Heat oil in a medium saucepan over medium heat. Add onion and sauté for 1 minute. Add bay leaf, star anise, lemon zest, salt, peppercorns, and coriander and fennel seeds and cook for 10 minutes, or until onion is softened and translucent. Add prawn shells, stir gently to coat and then cook for 10 minutes.

Stir in tomato paste, mix well and cook for another minute to lightly brown. Add tomato, then pour in white wine and bring to a quick simmer to evaporate the alcohol. Reduce heat to medium, add stock (or water) and simmer for 30 minutes, or until flavours have developed. Set aside to cool slightly.

Transfer mixture, including shells, to a high-speed blender or Vitamix and blend until smooth. Pass through a fine-mesh sieve and push down with the back of a ladle to extract flavour from the pulp of the puréed shells. Set stock aside and discard shells.

Bouillabaisse In a small saucepan, combine stock and vegetables and bring to a simmer over medium-high heat. Add salmon and white fish and season with salt and pepper. Cook for 1 minute, stirring occasionally, or until fish is just cooked through. Add prawns, scallops and mussels and simmer for 2 minutes, or until seafood is just cooked and mussels have opened. Discard any unopened mussels.

Rouille

2 slices French baguette

2 Tbsp extra-virgin olive oil, plus
  extra for brushing

2 Fire-Roasted Peppers (see here)

1 slice white bread

1 clove garlic, chopped

2 Tbsp Prawn Stock (see here)

Splash of Pernod or Ricard

Pinch of saffron

Pinch of sea salt

Pinch of ground white pepper

Fire-roasted peppers On a gas stove or barbecue, put peppers directly into the flame, rotating them until completely blackened. (Alternatively, set the oven to broil, place peppers on a baking sheet and rotate occasionally until blackened.) Place peppers in a mixing bowl, cover with plastic wrap or a plate and set aside until cooled. (The steam from the hot peppers helps to lift the skin and makes them easier to peel.) Using your fingers, peel off skin and remove seeds.

Rouille Preheat oven to 350°F.

Brush baguette slices with oil and toast in the oven for 4 to 6 minutes. Remove from oven and set aside.

In a food processor, blend fire-roasted peppers, bread, garlic, stock, Pernod (or Ricard), saffron, salt and white pepper until smooth. Slowly add 2 tablespoons oil until incorporated, then transfer to a small dish.

Assembly Remove bouillabaisse from the heat and transfer into soup bowls. Serve immediately with rouille and a side of toasted baguette.

Pictured | p. 79

Deane House
Matthias Fong

in the Restaurant category. And, like its sister restaurant, River Café (p. 164), Deane House contemplates the future of food and self-sufficient sustainability.

ABOUT THE CHEF

Executive chef Matthias Fong oversees two of the best kitchens in Calgary: those of Deane House and River Café. He spent his childhood hours in the kitchen, watching his mother and grandmother cook. While completing his studies at the University of Calgary, this Calgary-native worked at River Café—and developed a profound appreciation for the study of food.

He then worked at Michelin-starred Marcus (a Marcus Wareing restaurant), which specializes in contemporary British seasonal cuisine, before returning to River Café, where he discovered the potential for developing a Canadian cuisine. So he began to explore local and regional ingredients, especially those from the gardens surrounding the restaurant. "My hope has been to develop a distinctly contemporary Canadian cuisine through ingredients, history and culture," he says.

Fong's completely Canadian menu received University of Guelph's Good Food Innovation Award in 2017 and earned him a silver medal at Gold Medal Plates. His contribution has also helped River Café appear on best restaurant lists in *Avenue* and *Where Calgary* magazines, as well as Canada's 100 Best Restaurants list in 2016, 2017 and 2018.

Built in 1906, Deane House was revitalized and renovated by proprietor Sal Howell and her team, along with the City of Calgary and the Fort Calgary Preservation Society. Original rooms were perfectly restored and an airy, state-of-the-art kitchen built. With sweeping river views, banks of wild roses, spruce and elm, the bucolic setting complements a uniquely Canadian menu.

Deane House offers an impressive menu built around the history of the house, the land and the people. Popular dishes include succulent kombu-cured ling cod served with "Hannah glasses" curry, wild rice and Salt Spring Island mussels, and Albacore tuna with Saskatoon berry ponzu and bison pemmican. A multi-course tasting menu offers expertly navigated historical recipes with aplomb. In fact, in 2018, Deane House won the White Hat of the Year award

Soup

1 (2- to 3-lb) head paradox cabbage

3 Tbsp canola oil (divided)

Kosher salt, to taste

1 small yellow onion, chopped

1 small leek, white and light green parts only, sliced (½ cup)

¼ small Granny Smith apple, peeled and chopped

3 cloves garlic, finely chopped

1 Tbsp finely chopped shallot

1 star anise

1 cup dry white wine

6 cups vegetable stock

½ cup apple juice

1 tsp chopped thyme leaves, for garnish

1 loaf sourdough bread, sliced, to serve

Kale–camelina oil pistou

1 bunch black kale leaves, stems removed

½ cup camelina oil

Kosher salt, to taste

Serves 2 to 4

Paradox Cabbage Soup

This hearty, comforting soup is full of goodness—perfect to serve on a cold winter day. (Bonus: it's vegan-friendly and gluten-free.) Paradox cabbage is a dense variety of green cabbage that can be stored for an extended time in a cool, dark cellar. You can find it at local farmers' markets from October to May.

Soup Preheat oven to 350°F.

Rub the cabbage with 1½ tablespoons canola oil and season generously with salt. Place on a baking sheet and roast for 3 to 4 hours, until fork tender and the exterior leaves are burnt. Remove from oven and set aside to cool.

Peel off the burnt leaves and halve the cabbage. Cut out and discard the core. Chop cabbage into 1-inch chunks and set aside.

Heat the remaining 1½ tablespoons oil in a stockpot over medium-high heat. Add onion, leek, apple, garlic, shallot and star anise for 4 minutes, or until onions are softened and translucent.

Pour in wine and cook for 5 minutes, or until liquid is reduced by half. Add stock and apple juice and bring to a simmer. Stir in cabbage and simmer for 10 minutes. Discard star anise. Transfer mixture to a blender, working in batches if necessary, and purée until smooth. If necessary, add more stock to thin out the soup. Pass through a fine-mesh sieve. Repeat with the remaining batches. Season with salt and keep warm.

Kale–camelina oil pistou Fill a large bowl with ice water.

In a saucepan of salted water, cook kale for 1 minute. Drain, then transfer to the bowl of ice water to cool. Drain, squeeze out any excess water and transfer to a blender. With the motor running, gradually pour in oil, puréeing until smooth. Season with salt.

Assembly Stir pistou into the soup and heat through. Remove soup from heat (it will discolour if it cooks any longer) and serve immediately with a sprinkle of chopped thyme, and sourdough on the side.

▶ Haida Gwaii Halibut Cakes with Tartar Sauce | p. 86

Tartar sauce

½ cup mayonnaise

¼ cup chopped dill or gherkin pickles

1 tsp Worcestershire sauce

2 tsp freshly squeezed lemon juice

1 tsp grated lemon zest

1 tsp capers, chopped

¼ tsp chopped dill

2 tsp finely chopped shallots

1 tsp thinly sliced chives

2 anchovy fillets, chopped

½ tsp Marmite (optional)

½ tsp hot sauce of choice

½ tsp sherry vinegar

Kosher salt and freshly ground black pepper, to taste

Halibut cakes

2 large cloves garlic, crushed

3 bay leaves

2 large slices ginger

1 Tbsp kosher salt, plus extra to taste

1 lb yellow flesh or Russet potatoes, cut into 1-inch cubes

1 lb Haida Gwaii halibut, cut into 2-inch pieces

1 Tbsp canola oil

1 cup thinly sliced leeks

1 Tbsp chopped chervil

1 Tbsp thinly sliced chives

Grated zest and juice of ½ lemon

Breading

1 cup all-purpose flour

4 large eggs, beaten

3 cups panko crumbs

Assembly

½ cup canola oil

Light salad or roasted vegetables, to serve

Haida Gwaii Halibut Cakes with Tartar Sauce

Serves 6

Halibut has dense, firm-textured flesh that lends itself beautifully to this decadent brunch dish. If you want, make smaller cakes by rolling the halibut into firm balls the size of a golf ball and then flattening them out. The tangy and tasty tartar sauce can be made in advance and stored in the refrigerator. In fact, the entire recipe can be made the night before your brunch and refrigerated until needed.

Tartar sauce In a mixing bowl, combine all ingredients. Refrigerate until needed.

Halibut cakes Bring 2 litres water to a boil in a medium saucepan. Add garlic, bay leaves, ginger and salt. Reduce heat to medium-low and simmer. Add potatoes and cook for 7 minutes, or until tender. Strain, reserving the cooking water for the halibut. Set potatoes aside in a large mixing bowl and cover with a dish towel.

Bring the reserved potato water to a simmer. Add halibut and cook for 7 to 8 minutes, until cooked through. Drain halibut, discarding garlic, bay leaves, ginger and water. Gently stir halibut with the potatoes until the fish has broken into large flakes.

Heat oil in a small frying pan over medium heat. Add leeks and sauté for 5 to 7 minutes, until tender. Add leeks to the potato-halibut mixture. Stir in chervil, chives and lemon zest and juice. Using two forks, gently break up potatoes and fluff the mixture until the ingredients are evenly combined. Season with salt.

Form ¼ cup of the mixture into a firm patty, about 1 inch thick. Repeat with remaining mixture.

NOTE: Uncooked halibut cakes can be frozen. Lay them, evenly spaced apart, on a parchment-lined baking sheet. Cover and freeze overnight. Store them in an airtight container in the freezer for up to 1 month. To cook, simply thaw out and cook as instructed.

Breading Line a baking sheet with parchment paper. Line up three shallow bowls and place flour, eggs and panko crumbs in one each. Dip halibut cakes into flour, then into eggs and then into panko crumbs. Ensure an even crust by coating the entire surface area at each stage of breading. Place halibut cakes on the prepared baking sheet.

Assembly Preheat oven to 350°F.

Heat oil in a cast-iron skillet or ovenproof frying pan over medium-high heat. Add halibut cakes and cook for 2 minutes, or until golden. Turn and cook for another 2 minutes, or until golden on the second side. Put the pan in the oven and bake halibut cakes for 3 to 4 minutes, flipping occasionally.

Transfer halibut cakes to individual plates and serve with a generous scoop of the tartar sauce and salad or roasted vegetables.

Decadent Brulee
Pam Fortier

fans. It has a full selection: pies, cakes, tortes, tarts and (no surprise) show-stopping wedding cakes. For all your dessert needs, Decadent Brulee ought to be your port of call.

ABOUT THE BAKER

Pam Fortier discovered her love for baking when she attended SAIT's (Southern Alberta Institute of Technology's) culinary program. After a stint at the now-defunct restaurant Foodsmith, Fortier moved to Vancouver to take pastry and dessert courses at Dubrulle Culinary Arts, later returning to Calgary to work at The Cookbook Co. Cooks (p. 62), where she sold her pastries to catering companies. Fortier eventually took ownership of Decadent Desserts and Calgarians have been in love with her desserts ever since. Let us eat cake!

Decadent Brulee is the story of two bakeries made one. Back in the nineties, Decadent Desserts was one of Calgary's trendiest dessert spots. It was a popular date-night destination and always busy. In 2016, owner Pam Fortier purchased Brulee Bakery and moved Decadent Desserts into that location. It was like setting up house with two sets of furniture. Wanting to highlight Decadent's confections and preserve Brulee's signature desserts, Pam decided to offer both—and Decadent Brulee was born.

The bakery continues the tradition of baking from scratch, to the delight of existing and new

Crust

Cooking spray, for greasing

1½ cups (3 sticks) unsalted butter, softened

1 cup granulated sugar

4 cups all-purpose flour

¼ cup pecans, toasted and finely chopped

½ tsp kosher salt

Topping

2 cups packed brown sugar

½ cup (1 stick) unsalted butter, melted

½ cup corn syrup

½ cup maple syrup

1 tsp vanilla extract

½ tsp kosher salt

6 large eggs

2½ cups toasted pecans, finely chopped

¾ cup good-quality chocolate chips (preferably Callebaut)

1 cup dried chopped figs (about 4)

Dark chocolate, melted (optional)

Makes 24

Fig Pecan Triangles

These nut-laden, mouth-watering cookies are a fall favourite at Decadent Brulee, but they are delicious any time of year.

Crust Preheat oven to 375°F.

Spray an 11- × 17-inch baking sheet with cooking spray and line with parchment paper.

In a stand mixer fitted with the paddle attachment, cream butter and sugar. In a separate bowl, combine flour, pecans and salt. Add dry ingredients to butter mixture and mix well.

Press mixture onto the prepared baking sheet, patting to an even thickness. Bake for 10 to 12 minutes, or until lightly golden. Remove from oven and set aside to cool on the baking sheet.

Topping Preheat oven to 375°F.

In a large bowl, combine sugar, butter, both syrups, vanilla, salt and eggs, stirring to mix well. Stir in pecans, chocolate chips and figs. Pour mixture over crust and bake for 25 minutes, or until eggs are set. Remove from oven and set aside to cool.

Assembly Cut slab into 12 squares, then cut each diagonally to make 24 triangles. Dip edges in melted chocolate, if using, then set aside for 15 minutes. Dig in!

Meringue
⅔ cup cocoa powder
1½ cups icing sugar, plus extra
   for dusting
2 cups egg whites (about
   9 large eggs)
1⅔ cups granulated sugar
   (divided)

Chocolate mousse
1 lb good-quality dark chocolate,
   finely chopped
4 cups whipping cream

Serves
12 to 14

Concorde Cake

Created in the early seventies by renowned pastry chef Gaston Lenôtre, this gluten-free chocolate mousse cake was meant as a tribute to the famed Concorde plane. Make it a day in advance, as it will be easier to cut.

Meringue Preheat oven to 325°F. Place a piece of parchment paper on each of three baking sheets. Using a pencil, draw two 7-inch circles on the first sheet, and one 7-inch circle on the second. Turn parchment over so the meringue doesn't touch the pencil marks. Set aside the third baking sheet.

Sift cocoa and icing sugar into a bowl. In a stand mixer fitted with the whisk attachment, beat egg whites on medium speed until frothy. With the motor running, add 1 cup granulated sugar. Increase speed to high and whip mixture just until stiff peaks form. Reduce speed to low and add the remaining ⅔ cup granulated sugar. Using a rubber spatula, fold in the cocoa and icing sugar mixture.

Working quickly before it deflates, spoon meringue mixture into a piping bag fitted with a 1-inch tip.

Pipe a dollop of meringue mixture beneath the corners of the parchment paper on all baking sheets to "glue" down the parchment. Pipe mixture in a spiral motion to fill the circle outlines. Using the back of a spoon, fill in any gaps. Randomly pipe the remainder of the mixture on the third parchment-lined sheet. This does not need to be perfect, as it is going to be broken into bits for decoration. The meringues will expand as they bake.

Bake for 1½ hours. Turn off the heat and allow meringues to cool overnight in the oven.

Chocolate mousse Using a double boiler, melt chocolate. (Alternatively, melt in the microwave.) Set aside.

In a large bowl, whip cream to medium-stiff peaks. Add a quarter of the chocolate and quickly whisk by hand to incorporate. Add the remaining chocolate and whisk to combine.

Assembly Working immediately before it sets, use an offset spatula to dab mousse in the centre of a 10-inch cake pan as "glue." Place a meringue on top, then spread a ¾-inch-thick layer of mousse evenly overtop. Repeat with a second layer. Place the third layer on top and ice the entire cake with the remaining mousse.

Chop the meringue on the third baking sheet into ½-inch pieces. Place the pieces all over the sides and top of the cake. Dust with icing sugar. Place cake on a plate and serve.

Eau Claire Distillery
David Farran

that Eau Claire is developing seven acres of land, just behind the distillery, as a welcoming agro-tourism destination. With a focus on best farming practices, it will host special events, ranging from weddings and parties to long table dinners. It doesn't get any more local and if indeed today's rain is tomorrow's whiskey, then we're in for a treat.

ABOUT THE OWNER

Having grown up in a ranching and farming family, David Farran took a circuitous route back to the farm after graduating with an MBA from the University of Calgary. He started out as one of Big Rock Brewery's first employees and soon worked his way up to vice-president.

After that, a six-month sojourn in the west of New Guinea led to the formation of Pipestone Travel Outfitters—testimony to Farran's knack for transforming things that he loves into successful businesses. Following this, Farran led Associate Veterinary Clinics to become Canada's largest veterinary company. Starting Eau Claire Distillery in Turner Valley was a natural step because it combined his love of farming and of draft horses: the distillery's neighbouring field produces grain, which is collected by horse-drawn harvesters and used to produce craft distilled spirits. "Alberta farmers produce the best barley in the world," Farran tells us. "And it translates into extraordinary spirits from farm to glass."

If you happen to be driving through Turner Valley and see a four-horse team pulling an old-fashioned harvester, that would be Eau Claire Distillery bringing in its crop. Their farm-to-glass ethos starts in the field, resulting in spirits made with high-quality grains.

Housed in a converted 1929 movie theatre in Turner Valley, Eau Claire Distillery has a team of dedicated locals plus internationally trained master distillers producing award-winning handcrafted gin, vodka and whiskey.

The distillery also has a tasting room with bistro-style offerings. The menu features fresh, local food with fun vodka- and gin-infused options like "drunken meatballs" and "gin rummy & cheese," as well as house-made cocktails (pp. 93 and 95) using spirits distilled on premise.

Those who are serious about farm-to-table and farm-to-glass will be pleased to know

1½ oz Prickly Pear EquineOx
¾ oz freshly squeezed lime juice
2 to 3 sprigs mint
Lime slices
Eau Claire Soda Company Original
    Tonic Water or prosecco
Lime wheel, for garnish

Serves 1

Millarville Mojito

Whoever said that revenge is best served cold must have been referring to sipping an icy mojito in defiance of a hot day. Prickly Pear EquineOx is a sweet, barley-based alcohol that's perfect for this unique cocktail.

Place Prickly Pear EquineOx, lime juice, one sprig of mint and lime slices in a Boston shaker. Gently muddle, making sure to not shred or bruise the mint. (Discard the limes and any damaged mint and add a fresh sprig.) Pour mixture into a tall, ice-filled Tom Collins glass, top with tonic (or prosecco) and stir to combine.

Take a mint sprig and slap it between your hands to release the oils. Slide the sprig down the inside of the glass. Run the flesh of the lime wheel around the entire rim, then add it to the cocktail. Serve immediately.

Grande G and T
1 Tbsp fruity loose-leaf tea
    (preferably TotaliTea Sunshine
    Orange)
2 fl oz Eau Claire Parlour gin
Good-quality tonic water
Thin slice of orange peel or citrus
    peel of your choice

Percheron Negroni
1 fl oz Eau Claire Parlour gin
1 fl oz Campari
1 fl oz pyment (we use
    Fallentimber pyment)
Thin slice of orange peel or
    dried orange wheel

Serves 2

Eau Claire Parlour Gin Cocktails

A bespoke, well-made cocktail always has the capacity to make life seem a little better—and these drinks are no exception. The Grande G and T features gin, tonic water and loose-leaf tea, while the Percheron Negroni is enhanced with Campari and Fallentimber's pyment, a mead made with cabernet sauvignon grapes.

Grande G and T Place tea in a tea ball or reusable tea bag and put it in a snifter. Pour in gin and steep for 2 minutes. Remove the tea ball or bag, add an ice cube and top with tonic water. Gently stir.

Squeeze orange (or other citrus) peel lengthwise to extract the oils and rub over the rim of the glass. Drop in peel and enjoy!

Percheron Negroni Place a large ice cube (or 2 smaller ones) in a glass tumbler and pour in the gin, Campari and pyment. Stir. Squeeze orange peel lengthwise to extract the oils and rub over the rim of the glass. Drop in the peel (or dried orange wheel) and enjoy!

Empire Provisions

Karen Kho and Dave Sturies

Empire Provisions is the kind of little oasis you wished existed in every neighbourhood, especially your own. Located in Haysboro, this stylish, family-run emporium is dedicated to quality food, offering premium charcuterie, house-smoked specialties, fresh-made sandwiches and a large selection of cheeses and olives to take home. It also has an excellent coffee program.

For owners Karen Kho and Dave Sturies, Empire Provisions is an evolving labour of love. Sturies is the resident butcher and creates his own sausage recipes: on any given day, the deli features one to two dozen types of fresh sausages and 30 cured sausage varieties, from Esposito and chorizo to Burmese to Toulouse. The daily special, aptly titled Meat of the Moment, is alone often worth the trip.

And here's a bonus: catering is offered for both small and large gatherings. When it comes to meat, Empire Provisions is a smart, sleek and serious purveyor.

ABOUT THE OWNERS

Karen Kho, a certified sommelier, has an impressive resumé. She worked in retail wine sales at Bin 905 in 2001, was the wine director for Velvet at the GRAND, Cilantro (p. 56) and The Ranche, and created the wine program at Vin Room. Upon moving to Vancouver, she attended the Pacific Institute of Culinary Arts (PICA). Returning to Calgary, Kho started at Teatro Group in management, working her way up to operations manager.

Although Dave Sturies has a degree in environmental science, he's always held his own in a kitchen. He crafted his skills with a Calgary butcher and then moved to Teatro Ristorante. He then perfected his sausage-making skills at a shared commercial kitchen space, selling his products into retail stores and restaurants. As Kho says, "We basically started out with a small prep table and some shared fridge space."

In 2017, Kho and Sturies seized the opportunity to take over Cured (formerly the European Deli) in Haysboro, renamed it Empire Provisions, and turned their long-time dream into a reality.

¼ cup canola oil, plus extra
  if needed
2½ lbs pork shoulder, cut into
  2-inch cubes
1 large Spanish onion, coarsely
  chopped
3 heads garlic, cloves peeled
2 knobs ginger, peeled and
  thinly sliced (1 cup)

1 cup apple cider vinegar
1 cup rice vinegar
½ tsp black peppercorns
4 to 6 bay leaves
Kosher salt and freshly ground
  black pepper, to taste
Steamed rice, to serve (optional)
Extra-virgin olive oil, for drizzling
  (optional)

*Serves
4 to 6*

Karen's Pork Adobo

Homemade adobo is a Filipino staple typically prepared by memory, touch and taste—rarely is a recipe followed. Although the dish is traditionally made with chicken, Karen Kho uses pork to balance out the fat and vinegar. She also likes the way whole garlic, peppercorns and ginger cook down with the sauce, adding a hit of spice. This adobo would be incomplete without a bowl of steamed white rice to accompany it.

Heat oil in a Dutch oven over medium heat. Add pork shoulder, in batches, and sear each side for 10 minutes, or until browned. Transfer to a plate once seared, scooping out excess liquid from the pot with a large spoon between batches.

Heat oil in the same pot over medium heat (add more oil, if necessary). Add onion, garlic and ginger and sauté for 4 minutes, or until onion has softened. Stir in pork, both vinegars, peppercorns and bay leaves. The liquid should cover the meat. (Top up with more vinegar or water, if needed.) Bring to a simmer, cover and cook for 45 minutes. Remove lid and simmer for another 30 minutes, or until pork is fork tender.

Season with salt and pepper to taste. (If the sauce is too acidic, thin it out with water.) Using a spoon, skim off the fat on the surface of the sauce. Remove bay leaves and serve over generous portions of steamed rice, drizzled with olive oil, if using.

Pickled red onion

¾ cup red onion, thinly sliced
1 cup red wine vinegar

Lemon aioli

3 egg yolks
2 Tbsp freshly squeezed
   lemon juice
1 tsp Dijon mustard
½ tsp kosher salt
½ cup canola oil

Torta

2 Tbsp canola oil
4 Empire Provisions longanisa
   sausage, meat removed from
   casing
4 ciabatta buns, halved
12 thin slices Manchego
2 avocados, peeled, pitted and
   sliced lengthwise
6 Romaine lettuce leaves
½ cup torn cilantro leaves
Valentina hot sauce (optional)

Makes 4
sandwiches

Señor Torta

Señor Torta, also known as Mister Sandwich, is a creative take on Mexican street food. "The bright condiments make a nice contrast to the smoky richness of our longanisa sausage." Longanisa is a type of Mexican smoky sausage; at Empire Provisions, they make it with annatto, paprika, garlic and red wine vinegar. If you can't find longanisa, fresh chorizo is a good substitute.

Pickled red onion In a small non-reactive bowl, combine onion and vinegar. Cover and refrigerate for 4 to 12 hours to pickle.

Lemon aioli In a stand mixer fitted with the whisk attachment, combine egg yolks, lemon juice, mustard and salt and whisk on high speed. With the motor running, slowly add oil until mixture is emulsified. The aioli can be stored in a sealed container in the refrigerator for up to 5 days.

Torta Heat oil in a frying pan over medium heat. Crumble sausage meat into the pan and sauté for 6 to 8 minutes, until cooked through.

Slather aioli on the cut sides of ciabatta, then place ciabatta, cut side up, under the broiler and toast. (Alternatively, place it cut side down in a hot frying pan to toast.)

Gather the sausage meat in the pan. Layer Manchego slices on top and cook until cheese is melted. Using a flat spatula, divide mixture among the four ciabatta bun bottoms.

Layer avocado slices, pickled onion and lettuce on top. Finish with cilantro, a drizzle of aioli and hot sauce, if using.

Foreign Concept
Duncan Ly and Jinhee Lee

ABOUT THE CHEFS

As one of Calgary's most well-regarded chefs, Duncan Ly is a culinary maven who creates fusion food that's as sustainable as it is stunning. The award-winning chef has an expansive career and he honed his skills at the country's best: Tofino's Wickaninnish Inn and Calgary's Catch, Hotel Arts, and Kensington Riverside Inn. He was also culinary director for The Vintage Group. No stranger to competition, he represented Calgary at the Canadian Culinary Championships in 2014 and since then has mentored many young chefs.

Jinhee Lee, who leads the team at Foreign Concept, has acquired a reputation for inventive and flawlessly executed dishes. The talented executive chef won the gold at Gold Medal Plates in 2016 and 2017 and placed third on *Top Chef Canada* 2018. In fact, she was named one of *Avenue Calgary*'s 2016 "Top 5 people to watch in Calgary's food scene."

Thanks to Ly's Chinese-Vietnamese heritage and Canadian upbringing, and to Lee's Korean background, you can expect delicious combinations of familiar ingredients infused with bright, bold Asian flavours.

Chef Duncan Ly took a chance in 2016, leaving the security and ready accolades of the successful Hotel Arts restaurants (pp. 152, 158 and 216), where for 10 years he resided as executive chef, to open his own restaurant. "I love being in control of my own destiny, my own direction," he says. "This is my passion and a labour of love."

Cue in Foreign Concept, a restaurant which reflects Ly's food philosophy and offers top-notch sharing plates. Go for the Asian-inspired charcuterie or the skillfully prepared plates such as the refreshing butternut squash and green mango slaw and 72-hour sous-vide beef short ribs. Or better yet, be brave and make his signature dishes at home—his Alberta Trout Chả Cá Lã Vọng (p. 101) is *that* good.

Nước chấm (Vietnamese dipping sauce)

1 cup granulated sugar
½ cup fish sauce
2 cloves garlic, finely chopped
2 Tbsp freshly squeezed lime juice
½ red Thai chili, seeded, deveined and thinly sliced (optional)

Alberta trout Chả Cá Lã Vọng

1 cup yogurt
1 Tbsp ground turmeric
2 lbs Alberta rainbow trout fillets, skin on and cut into 3-inch pieces
1 package vermicelli rice noodles
Rice flour, for coating
3 Tbsp vegetable oil
2 Tbsp unsalted butter

2 large cloves garlic, chopped
1 bunch dill, chopped, plus extra for garnish
1 bunch green onions, cut into 2-inch lengths, plus extra for garnish
Peanuts, for garnish
Prawn crackers, for garnish (optional)

Alberta Trout Chả Cá Lã Vọng

Serves 4

This traditional Vietnamese dish is named after a Hanoi street called Chả Cá and the resident Lã Vọng, who created it. It is typically made with a local catfish, but here we use firm yet delicate Alberta rainbow trout, which takes on the savoury, fragrant and slightly tart umami notes beautifully. We recommend marinating the fish a day in advance and preparing the dipping sauce just before frying the fish.

Nước chấm (Vietnamese dipping sauce)
In a small saucepan, combine sugar, fish sauce and garlic. Stir in 1½ cups water and bring mixture to a simmer. Remove from heat and add lime juice and chili, if using. Chill before serving.

Alberta trout Chả Cá Lã Vọng In a large bowl, stir together yogurt and turmeric to combine. Add trout and toss to coat. Cover and marinate for at least 1 hour at room temperature, but preferably overnight in the refrigerator.

Cook vermicelli according to the package instructions and set aside.

Preheat a large frying pan over high heat. Remove trout from marinade, pat dry and discard marinade. Dredge trout in rice flour, dusting off any excess flour.

Add oil to the pan. Add trout, skin side down, and cook for 2 minutes, or until skin is golden and crispy. Flip fish over, then add butter, garlic, dill and green onions. Baste trout with the butter and cook for another minute. Remove from heat and keep warm.

Transfer vermicelli to a serving platter, arrange trout fillets on top and pour butter mixture over fish.

Garnish with dill, green onions and peanuts. Serve family-style with more peanuts, prawn crackers, if using, and Nước chấm dipping sauce.

Chowder base

2 Tbsp unsalted butter

2 stalks lemongrass, coarsely chopped

1 small piece ginger, peeled and coarsely chopped

1 large carrot, coarsely chopped

4 stalks celery, coarsely chopped

1 large yellow onion, coarsely chopped

1 leek, white part only, thinly sliced

1 head garlic, cloves separated, peeled and coarsely chopped

1 red kuri squash, peeled, seeded and cut into 1-inch cubes

4 cups chicken stock

4 cups coconut milk

1 Tbsp Thai red curry paste

Juice of 3 limes

1 Tbsp fish sauce

Kosher salt and ground white pepper, to taste

Kuri squash and seafood chowder

½ red kuri squash, peeled, seeded, and cut into 1-inch cubes

2 large potatoes, cut into 1-inch cubes

8 patty pan squash, quartered

8 kohlrabi, peeled and chopped

½ cup pearl onions

1 lb live mussels, scrubbed clean

8 oz spot prawns

8 oz ocean halibut, cut into 1-inch cubes

¼ cup whipping cream

Chives, chopped, for garnish

Extra-virgin olive oil, for drizzling

Kuri Squash and Seafood Chowder

Serves 8 to 10

Red kuri squash is a thin-skinned and pear-shaped orange winter squash that looks like a small pumpkin. When cooked, the golden flesh is smooth, sweet and rich. This hearty chowder pairs Southeast Asian and Canadian flavours for a thoroughly satisfying and nourishing meal when the temperature drops.

Chowder base Melt butter in a large stockpot over medium heat. Add lemongrass, ginger, carrot, celery, onion, leek and garlic, then reduce heat to low. Sauté for 15 to 20 minutes, until vegetables are tender. Add squash and cook for another 10 minutes.

Pour in chicken stock and bring to a boil over high heat. Reduce heat to medium and simmer for 10 minutes. Add coconut milk and curry paste and simmer for another 15 minutes.

Transfer chowder to a blender and purée until smooth and creamy. Strain through a fine-mesh sieve, then stir in lime juice and fish sauce. Season with salt and white pepper.

Kuri squash and seafood chowder Bring chowder base to a boil. Add squash, potatoes, patty pan squash, kohlrabi and onions. Cook for 15 minutes, or until vegetables are tender.

Add mussels, prawns and halibut and cook for 10 minutes, or until mussels open and seafood is cooked. Discard any unopened mussels. Stir in cream and cook for 1 minute.

Serve chowder in bowls topped with chives and a drizzle of olive oil.

KLEIN / HARRIS

Christina Mah and James Waters

Constructed in 1891, the J.H. Ashdown Hardware Company building is one of Stephen Avenue's oldest buildings. In 2016, owners Suzanne Baden and Lyle Furber partnered with cocktail curator Christina Mah and executive chef James Waters to form KLEIN / HARRIS, a restaurant committed to True North cuisine and which calls the former hardware building home.

This is casual dining at its finest, highlighting quality meat, fish and produce. Waters's culinary style draws inspiration from home-grown produce: think prime and AAA-grade Alberta beef; chanterelles, morels, porcini and B.C. lobster mushrooms; and P.E.I. Malpeque oysters. With dishes like heritage greens with grated carrot, cucumber, shaved radish, celery, roasted red pepper and cider vinaigrette, or crispy pork loin served with baby potatoes, screech-roasted beets and apples, and a smoked onion and mustard reduction, the menu is a tantalizing feast for the eyes and taste buds.

And mix master Christina Mah creates cocktails with real skill. Her Caesar with house-made Caesar broth has transformative powers, while the smoked spruce Collins is a knockout original with Canadian-driven ingredients. In fact, the entire program is driven by regional products: Eau Claire Distillery's spirits (p. 92) and wines from Vineland, Ontario, and Oliver, B.C.

ABOUT THE DUO

Cocktail curator Christina Mah is one busy woman. She honed her skills over the years by creating uniquely Canadian libations, and it's paid off. Her innovative cocktails have won her accolades—one at the Calgary Cocktail Challenge and another at the Grey Goose Pour Masters. There was also that time she bartended at the prestigious Tales of the Cocktail on tour in Vancouver. And if that weren't enough, she also happens to be former president of Canadian Professional Bartenders

Association's Alberta chapter and has collaborated with Alberta Culinary Tourism Alliance and Beakerhead. Without any shadow of a doubt, Mah is winning at cocktails.

Self-taught chef James Waters has been around the block, so to speak. He's worked in chain restaurants and at Hotel Arts and Cravings Market and has consulted on menus at two of Calgary's most beloved restaurants, Diner Deluxe and Ship & Anchor. It was when he was working at Spruce Meadows that he met his future business and life partner, Christina Mah. Their break came in 2013, when Waters was executive chef at Home Tasting Room. In 2016, Mah and Waters proposed an idea for a new concept and within 28 business days KLEIN / HARRIS was born.

KLEIN / HARRIS Caesar broth

2 large yellow or green tomatoes

2 bunches celery, chopped

1 to 1½ fresh jalapeño peppers,
depending on your heat preference

4 cups clam nectar

1½ cups apple cider vinegar

1 cup granulated sugar

1 Tbsp kosher salt

Pickled celery and carrot

2 cloves garlic

3 bay leaves

1 sprig thyme

¾ cup white vinegar

2¼ Tbsp granulated sugar

1½ Tbsp kosher salt

2 stalks celery, cut into thin
3-inch-long strips

2 large purple carrots, cut into
thin 3-inch-long strips

Caesar

1½ fl oz vodka or gin

3 oz Caesar Broth (see here)

¼ fl oz freshly squeezed lime juice

2 slices yellow or green tomato,
for garnish

Serves 4

KLEIN / HARRIS Caesar

The Caesar was invented in 1969 at the Calgary Inn (now the Westin Hotel). Since then, this brunch-friendly cocktail has been occasionally described as "steak in a glass." Sweet, tangy, savoury and immensely satisfying, the secret to Christina Mah's version is its briny homemade broth.

KLEIN / HARRIS Caesar broth In a blender, blend all ingredients at high speed until smooth. (Work in batches, if necessary.) Strain through a fine-mesh sieve or a jelly bag. (The liquid should be completely smooth—strain again if necessary.)

Pour the strained liquid into a saucepan and bring to a boil. Remove from heat. Set aside to cool, then store in a sealed container in the refrigerator for up to 1 week. It can also be made ahead of time and frozen in portions. Use within 3 weeks, thawing when needed.

Pickled celery and carrot Place an empty 1-quart Mason jar, open side up, on a rack in a large saucepan or canner. Fill saucepan with enough water to cover the jar by 1 inch and boil for 10 minutes. Carefully remove the jar from the boiling water, drain and place on a wire rack to cool. Be very careful: the jar will be hot! Be sure to keep the work area clean during the pickling process—dirt may contain harmful bacteria.

In a large saucepan, combine garlic, bay leaves, thyme, vinegar, sugar and salt. Pour in 1¼ cups water, bring to a boil and boil until sugar and salt are dissolved.

Put celery and carrots in the sterilized jar, then pour in pickling mixture. Set aside to cool. The pickled vegetables can be stored, sealed, in the refrigerator for up to 2 weeks.

Caesar Combine all ingredients except tomato in a Tom Collins glass, add ice and stir.

To serve Top up with fresh ice and garnish with pickled celery and carrot. Angle tomato slices against the side of the glass (the garnish and ice cubes will hold them in place) or skewer them.

Seared diver scallops
1 lb fresh or frozen and
  thawed diver scallops

Fire-roasted red pepper
2 red bell peppers

Apple broth
1 onion, thinly sliced
2 cloves garlic
2 cups apple juice
¼ cup apple cider vinegar
2 Tbsp liquid smoke
2 Granny Smith apples, peeled,
  cored and coarsely chopped

Assembly
Kosher salt, to taste
2 Tbsp olive oil, plus extra for searing
8 oz thick-cut or slab bacon,
  cut into ¼-inch cubes
1 head Savoy cabbage, shredded
  (4 cups)
1 cup vegetable stock
1 Tbsp finely chopped chives,
  plus extra for sprinkling
Chive flowers, for garnish
Maldon salt, for sprinkling

Seared Diver Scallops with Bacon-Laced Cabbage and Apple Broth

Serves 4

Sweet, fresh diver scallops are delicious and easy to cook. Pair with crispy bacon lardons, cabbage, red pepper and apple broth and you have a simple yet robust meal. Roast the red peppers on high heat so that the skin can be removed without cooking the pepper too much.

Seared diver scallops Using a paring knife, carefully dislodge any visible side muscle from the scallops, then pull it away and discard. (The muscle is tough and unpleasant to eat.) Place cleaned scallops on a large plate lined with paper towel, then place paper towel on top. Put a baking sheet on top to weigh it down slightly and refrigerate for 15 minutes (and up to 1 hour).

Fire-roasted red pepper On a gas stove, put peppers directly into the flame, rotating them until completely blackened. (Alternatively, set an oven to broil. Roast peppers on a baking sheet and rotate occasionally until blackened.) Place peppers in a mixing bowl, cover with plastic wrap or a plate and set aside until cooled. (The steam from the hot peppers helps to lift the skin and makes them easier to peel.) Using your fingers, peel off skin and remove seeds. Finely chop peppers and set aside for later use.

Apple broth In a large saucepan, combine onion, garlic, apple juice, vinegar and liquid smoke and bring to a boil. Boil for 3 minutes, or until onion is softened. (You don't want to reduce it.)

Purée apples in a blender until smooth. Slowly pour in the hot liquid to partially "cook" the apples with its heat. (Be careful not to splatter the liquid, as it's extremely hot.) Using a fine-mesh strainer, strain mixture into a bowl, cover to keep warm and set aside. Discard solids.

Assembly Set aside scallops at room temperature for 10 minutes. Season both sides with salt.

Heat oil in a frying pan over medium-high heat. Add bacon and cook for 3 to 5 minutes, until rendered and slightly browned. Add cabbage and sauté for 3 minutes, or until softened. Pour in vegetable stock and simmer for 3 minutes, or until heated through. Stir in roasted peppers and chives. Set aside and keep warm.

Into another frying pan, pour enough oil to cover the bottom and heat over high heat until nearly smoking. Carefully add scallops and sear, uncovered and untouched, for 2 minutes, or until a brown crust begins to form. Carefully flip scallops and cook for 30 seconds. Immediately transfer to a plate to prevent them from overcooking.

Pour apple broth onto a large platter. Place cabbage mixture overtop, then top with seared scallops.

Sprinkle the dish with chives or chive flowers and Maldon salt.

Knifewear
Kevin Kent

knives and plans are underway to open stores in Toronto and Kyoto, Japan.

"A great knife inspires your cooking and gives you something to look forward to," explains Kent. "A dull knife can ruin your whole month or more." He refuses to divulge the number of Japanese knives he owns, but it's a lot.

ABOUT THE CHEF

When Kevin Kent was seven years old, his uncle gave him a pocket knife, saying, "Don't tell your mom." To this day, knives have been Kent's obsession.

Kent honed his craft at River Café in Calgary and then moved to London, England, in 2001 to work for Fergus Henderson at St. John Restaurant. While there, Kent bought his first Japanese knife and was blown away. When he returned to Canada, he began selling Japanese kitchen knives from his backpack and Knifewear was born.

Not one to remain still, Kent has produced two award-winning films (*Springhammer* and *Springhammer 2*), has written a book titled *The Knifenerd Guide to Japanese Knives* and opened Kent of Inglewood, where you can find a complete range of traditional shaving gear and more: straight razors, safety razors, shave brushes, pomades, soaps and axes. Er, why you ask? Kent likes sharp stuff.

Chefs have been known to describe their knives as an extension of their body, and the most serious chefs swear by Japanese knives. Just the words *Japanese Damascus steel* will make the most ardent knife nerds swoon.

Which is why chefs, knife lovers and cooks in the know flock to Knifewear. Since 2007, Knifewear has cultivated personal relationships with master blacksmiths in Japan to promote and sell some of the best knives in the world—from groundbreakers such as Teruyasu Fujiwara to Moritaka blacksmiths, whose traditions stretch back 27 generations.

"We started the knife shops with the idea that New Knife Day should be the best day of the year," says founder Kevin Kent. Five shops later, Kent is still just as obsessed with Japanese

7 mini cucumbers or 1 English
   cucumber
1 tsp kosher salt
½ tsp sesame oil

Serves 6
(as a side)

Crunchy Cucumber Salad

In Japan during the hot summer months, salads and cold noodle dishes are commonly served with ice cubes to keep them cool and refreshing, and it makes for an unexpected and unique garnish that Kevin Kent loves serving with food. This crisp and refreshing salad is a fantastic foil to the Grilled Pork Belly Skewers (p. 112). Ironically, this Knifewear recipe doesn't require the use of a knife: just bash the cucumber until it breaks apart. Mini cucumbers are perfectly textured for this salad, but if you use a larger cucumber, remove most of the seeds to maintain optimal crunchiness.

Using a rolling pin, gently whack cucumbers so that they crack. (Use some control so they don't splatter across your kitchen; this may take a bit of practice.) Break cucumbers apart with your hands.

In a large bowl, sprinkle cucumbers with salt and set aside for 30 to 60 minutes, tossing every 15 minutes. Give cucumbers a quick rinse, then stir in sesame oil.

Serve with a few ice cubes to keep the dish cool.

Pictured | p. 113

5 to 6 bamboo skewers
(preferably 6-inch)

2½ lbs pork belly, skin removed

Kosher salt

Togarashi, to serve

Yuzu kosho, to serve

Crunchy Cucumber Salad
(p. 111), to serve

Grilled Pork Belly Skewers (or Fatty Meat on a Stick)

Makes 6 skewers

This recipe was inspired by Kevin Kent's most favourite restaurant in the world, "the fatty meat on a stick joint." Here, pork belly is cut into domino-sized pieces, generously seasoned with salt, then skewered and grilled. All the specialty ingredients, such as the *togarashi* (a Japanese spice blend of spicy pepper, sesame seeds and dried orange rind) and *yuzu kosho* (a chili and yuzu citrus paste), can be found at Korean and Japanese food stores. Cold sake is a natural drink pairing, but Dandy Brewing Company's Une Vieille Maîtresse Grisette would be an exceptional accompaniment.

Soak skewers in water for 20 minutes.

Meanwhile, cut pork belly lengthwise into 3-inch-wide strips and then cut the strips crosswise into 1-inch pieces. You are aiming for a piece the size of a domino. (The thicker the slice, the chewier the pork; the thinner the slice, the crispier.) Lay out 4 to 5 pieces on a cutting board and skewer them.

Preheat a grill. You can use any charcoal you like, including *binchō-tan* (white charcoal), wood coals or gas.

Generously season pork belly with salt. Place pork belly pieces, in batches, on the grill and move them around to avoid flame flare-up (which will create an unpleasant flavour).

Cook for 1 to 4 minutes on each side, or until browned on both sides and cooked through (depending on your preference for crispiness). Transfer to a plate and serve with togarashi, yuzu kosho and cucumber salad.

The Lake House
Gareth Colville

highlight the regional flavours of Western Canada, courtesy of Chef Gareth Colville and his award-winning team. Oh, and their eggs benny are possibly the best in the city (the hollandaise will call your name).

In fact, the top-notch food and service and large lakefront patio explain why The Lake House is one of Calgary's most popular wedding venues—you won't get any closer to nature in the city.

ABOUT THE CHEF

Chef Gareth Colville, originally from Norfolk, England, began cooking at a young age to help around the house. When his older brother began working as a chef in a local restaurant, Colville followed in his footsteps and became more involved in the culinary world. He moved to Canada and took his first Canadian chef position at The Ranche. "Cooking has always been my passion, but it truly came alive when I joined the CRMR family," he says.

In 2014, Colville moved to The Lake House and was later promoted to head chef. His seasonal menus incorporate elk and bison from Canadian Rocky Mountain Ranch and fresh produce from local farmers and producers. "Delighting guests who walk through our doors makes my job stand out and will always drive my passion for food," says Colville.

We Calgarians don't take lakeside dining for granted.

Built up and out over the water of Lake Bonavista, The Lake House feels like a mountain lodge retreat, with its sun-drenched dining room's stone fireplace, elk-antler chandeliers and a glass-encased wine cellar. The refurbished 19th-century bar is stocked with well-considered wines. Patrons take their seats in the upstairs dining room to enjoy satisfying libations like bourbon lemonade while admiring lakeside views.

Dishes such as the Rocky Mountain charcuterie board, pan-seared steelhead trout with blood-orange emulsion, and grilled wild boar chops are just some of the dishes that

Braised lamb leg

1 Tbsp kosher salt, plus extra
   to taste
1 tsp freshly ground black pepper,
   plus extra to taste
1 tsp ground nutmeg
½ tsp ground cinnamon
2 to 3 lbs boneless lamb leg, fat
   trimmed and cut into 6 pieces
2 Tbsp extra-virgin olive oil

1 onion, coarsely chopped
1 carrot, coarsely chopped
2 stalks celery, coarsely chopped
3 cloves garlic, crushed
1 cup full-bodied red wine,
   such as shiraz
¼ cup tomato paste
1 sprig rosemary
4 cups lamb or beef stock

Moussaka

2 large or 3 small eggplants, cut
   lengthwise into slices ¼-inch thick
1 Tbsp kosher salt, plus extra to taste
¼ cup olive oil
½ cup (1 stick) unsalted butter
7 Tbsp all-purpose flour
4 cups whole milk
Ground white pepper, to taste
2 egg yolks
2 cups grated Parmesan

Braised Lamb Leg Moussaka

Serves 6 to 8

Rich and savoury moussaka makes for a hearty and comforting meal on chilly days. The moussaka can be prepared a day in advance, and if you're making the béchamel at the same time, lay a sheet of plastic or waxed paper directly on top to prevent a skin from forming and keep it in the refrigerator. The lamb and stock can also be prepared up to this point a day in advance and stored in the refrigerator until needed. The added bonus is that the fat will harden, making it easier to remove.

The Lake House serves this dish with Parmesan-Crusted Lamb Rack (p. 119) for a double hit of lamb.

Braised lamb leg Preheat oven to 325°F.

In a small bowl, combine salt, pepper, nutmeg and cinnamon. Rub lamb with spice mixture. Heat oil in a large frying pan over medium-high heat. Add lamb and sear for 5 minutes on each side. Transfer to a roasting pan and set aside.

In the same frying pan, add onion, carrot, celery and garlic and sauté for 5 minutes, or until slightly softened.

Pour in wine and deglaze the pan. Add tomato paste, rosemary and stock. Season with salt and pepper and simmer for 5 minutes. Spoon vegetable mixture on top of the meat. Cover with aluminum foil and cook for 3 hours, or until the lamb falls off the bone. Remove from oven and set aside to cool slightly.

Transfer lamb meat to a bowl. Tear meat into small pieces and set aside.

Braising stock Skim off as much of the excess surface fat from the liquid remaining in the roasting pan as possible. Strain stock into a large saucepan, discarding the vegetables.

Heat stock over medium-high heat until reduced to 1½ cups. Add lamb to pan and set aside.

Moussaka Lay eggplant slices on paper towel and sprinkle lightly with salt. Set aside for 30 minutes to draw out the moisture.

Heat 1 tablespoon oil in a frying pan over high heat. Add eggplant slices, being careful to not overcrowd, and fry for 5 minutes, or until lightly browned. Flip and cook for another few minutes until lightly browned on the other side. Set aside on paper towel. Repeat until all the eggplant is cooked, adding more oil to the pan for each batch.

To make the béchamel, melt butter in a saucepan over medium heat. Stir in flour and cook for 5 minutes to cook out the raw taste. Reduce heat to medium-low and whisk in milk, continuing to whisk until mixture is thickened. Season with salt and pepper. Set aside to cool slightly and then gradually whisk in the egg yolks.

Preheat oven to 375°F.

In a 9- × 13-inch dish, arrange half the fried eggplant. Cover eggplant with half the lamb mixture, a few ladles of béchamel and half the Parmesan. Repeat eggplant and lamb layers once more, then finish with the rest of the béchamel and cheese on top.

Cover with aluminum foil and bake for 1½ hours. Remove foil and bake for another 10 minutes, or until cheese is browned.

Divide into portions and serve on individual plates. Serve immediately.

Parmesan-crusted lamb rack

2 Tbsp olive oil

2 racks of lamb, 8 points per rack, Frenched

1 tsp kosher salt

1 tsp freshly ground black pepper

3 Tbsp panko crumbs

2 Tbsp freshly grated Parmesan

1 Tbsp chopped oregano

1 Tbsp Dijon mustard

Roasted seasonal vegetables, to serve (optional)

Oregano oil

¼ cup extra-virgin olive oil

2 tsp chopped oregano

Tomato emulsion

6 tomatoes, cut into wedges

2 cloves garlic

2 Tbsp extra-virgin olive oil

1 tsp red wine vinegar

1 tsp granulated sugar

1 Tbsp tomato paste

Kosher salt and freshly ground black pepper, to taste

Serves 4 to 6

Parmesan-Crusted Lamb Rack

Alberta lamb is tender, juicy and mild, thanks to a free-range diet of grasses in the summer and alfalfa and grains in the fall. The rack of lamb naturally complements moussaka (p. 116) and, together, they create a year-round dish combo that draws inspiration from both the Mediterranean and Canada. Plus it's a comforting and warming dish on cold nights.

Parmesan-crusted lamb rack Preheat oven to 375°F.

Heat oil in a frying pan over high heat. Rub lamb with salt and pepper, add to pan and sear for 10 minutes, or until slightly browned on all sides. Using tongs, transfer lamb to a roasting pan and roast for around 15 minutes, for medium. Remove lamb and set aside for 10 minutes to rest. Keep the oven on.

Meanwhile, in a bowl, combine panko crumbs, Parmesan and oregano.

Smear mustard over lamb, then dredge in the panko mixture. Roast for 2½ minutes, or until crust has slightly browned.

Oregano oil Combine oil and oregano in a small bowl. Set aside.

Tomato emulsion Preheat oven to 375°F.

In a bowl, combine tomatoes, garlic and oil, tossing tomatoes to coat well. Spread tomatoes on a baking sheet and roast for 20 minutes, or until slightly brown and deflated. Set aside to cool.

Transfer tomatoes to a blender, add the remaining ingredients and blend until smooth. Season with salt and pepper. Transfer to a bowl and set aside.

Assembly Cut racks of lamb into single chops if serving six and into double chops if serving four.

Spoon tomato emulsion around lamb and drizzle oregano oil over the plate. Serve with roasted seasonal vegetables, if using.

MARKET
Evan Robertson

result, most items on the menu can be prepared gluten-free.

We're talking popcorn fried in bacon fat and finished with lashings of truffle oil, and poutine topped with 4K Farms pulled pork, poutine jus, cheese curds and house-cultivated pea shoots. The eggs benny is decked out with that same pulled pork, house-smoked bacon, crispy onions, pork jus and hollandaise on fresh focaccia.

MARKET supports animal welfare by donating a portion of its sales to the Alberta Animal Rescue Crew Society.

ABOUT THE CHEF

Executive chef Evan Robertson obtained his Red Seal certificate from Northern Alberta Institute of Technology. After graduation, he worked at Edmonton's Hardware Grill, followed by a return to the West Coast and the kitchens of Victoria's Aerie Resort and Ferris' Upstairs and Oyster Bar. Moving to Calgary, he eventually became the executive chef at The Pig and Duke, one of Canada's best gastropubs (and featured on the Food Network's popular TV series *You Gotta Eat Here!*). He joined MARKET's team in 2016.

"We've established relationships with our local farmers and suppliers, and I want to honour the products that I use," explains Robertson. "Chefs should respect the importance of the farmers who get up at 4 a.m. to start their daily chores."

We take pride in the fact that so many of our restaurants support sustainability and local community, and MARKET is no exception. But what sets them apart from the pack is that they take full control of their offerings. They bake bread daily and grow microgreens and select vegetables year-round. MARKET only uses Ocean Wise seafood and, to ensure no waste, meat is butchered nose to tail.

Founder Vanessa Salopek has been passionate about farm life and sustainability since spending her childhood summers at her grandparents' farm. After she was diagnosed with celiac disease, she made it her goal to provide fellow celiacs with a safe place to dine without compromising quality or taste. As a

▶ Duck Confit Pot Pie | p. 122

Herb salt

¼ cup kosher salt

¼ cup chopped Italian parsley

2 Tbsp packed brown sugar

2 Tbsp thyme leaves

1 tsp freshly ground black pepper

2 bay leaves

Duck confit

12 cloves garlic

4 duck legs

¼ cup Herb Salt (see here, divided)

5 cups rendered duck fat

Truffle cream sauce

2 Tbsp unsalted butter

1 yellow onion, chopped

4 cloves garlic, finely chopped

6 cremini mushrooms, stems removed and caps sliced ¼ inch thick

Kosher salt and freshly ground black pepper, to taste

½ cup chicken stock

2 cups whipping cream

1 Tbsp truffle oil

Duck confit pot pie filling

½ cup reserved duck confit jus or chicken stock

1 small red onion, chopped

1 small yellow onion, chopped

1 large carrot, chopped

3 stalks celery, chopped

¼ cup peas

4 cloves garlic, finely chopped

1 cup duck confit meat, shredded into bite-sized pieces

Truffle Cream Sauce (see here)

2 Tbsp fresh tarragon, chopped

Serves 4

Duck Confit Pot Pie

Age-old preservation techniques are introduced to a classic duck confit. Start a day in advance, as the duck legs need to be refrigerated for 24 hours after being rubbed with salt. If you would like to skip this step, purchase pre-made duck confit from a specialty food store.

Herb salt Place all ingredients in a food processor and blitz until well combined. Set aside in a small bowl.

Duck confit In a mini blender or food processor, purée garlic. Set aside.

Using scissors or a sharp knife, trim excess skin off the bottom of duck legs and around the edges, leaving at least ¼-inch overhang. Rub 1 tablespoon herb salt and 1 tablespoon garlic purée into each leg, adding a little extra over the thigh joint. Loosely cover with plastic wrap and refrigerate for 24 hours.

Preheat oven to 225°F. Rinse duck legs under cold running water to remove salt, then thoroughly pat dry.

Place duck legs in a roasting pan, skin side up, and pour in duck fat, ensuring that legs are submerged. Cook uncovered for 4 hours. Remove pan from the oven and set aside.

Strain fat through a fine-mesh sieve into a non-reactive container. As it solidifies, the meat juices will settle to the bottom. Carefully separate the fat from the juices. Set jus aside and reserve duck fat for future use (such as roasting potatoes).

Truffle cream sauce Melt butter in a frying pan over medium heat. Add onion and garlic and sauté for 5 minutes, or until softened. Add mushrooms and cook for 8 to 10 minutes, until mushrooms start to soften and release moisture. Season with salt and pepper.

Assembly

1 package frozen puff pastry, thawed

1 large egg, beaten

Kosher salt, to taste

1 tsp finely chopped chives or chive flowers, for garnish (optional)

Side salad, to serve

Pour in stock and cream and cook for 8 to 10 minutes, until reduced by half and mixture is a thick, creamy consistency. Stir in truffle oil. (The sauce can be prepared a day in advance. Refrigerate until needed and warm through before use.)

Duck confit pot pie filling Heat duck confit jus (or chicken stock) in a saucepan over medium heat. Add onion, carrot and celery and cook for 5 minutes, or until firm but not crunchy. Add peas and garlic and cook for another 5 minutes. Remove from heat and stir in duck confit, truffle cream sauce and tarragon. Transfer mixture to a casserole dish. (Filling can also be prepared in advance and set aside until you are ready to assemble and bake the final dish.)

Assembly Preheat oven to 425°F. Roll out and cut a sheet of puff pastry slightly larger than the casserole dish.

Fill dish with warm pot pie filling and place puff pastry overtop. Using a pastry brush, brush the puff pastry top with beaten egg and sprinkle with salt. Pierce the top with a fork to allow steam to escape while cooking. Bake for 15 minutes, or until pastry is golden and thoroughly cooked. Remove from oven and allow to cool slightly before serving.

Serve on individual plates, garnished with chives (or chive flowers), with a side of salad. It is also delicious cold with Dijon mustard or chutney.

Pictured | p. 121

Corn dog dipping sauce
½ cup rice vinegar
½ cup fish sauce
¼ cup granulated sugar
¼ cup freshly squeezed lime juice
1 Tbsp red chili flakes
2 cloves garlic, finely chopped

Wakame seaweed salad
1 oz dried wakame seaweed
1 cup hot green tea
4 green onions, sliced
2 carrots, shredded
¼ cup rice vinegar
¼ cup soy sauce
2 Tbsp sesame oil
1 Tbsp granulated sugar
1 Tbsp ginger purée
1 Tbsp garlic purée
1 tsp red chili flakes
2 Tbsp sesame seeds, toasted

Crab and shrimp sausage
8 oz shrimp, peeled and deveined
⅓ cup whipping cream
1 tsp lobster paste
1 lb crabmeat, shells removed
¼ cup finely chopped chives
1 tsp freshly ground black pepper

Crab Corn Dogs with Wakame Seaweed Salad

Serves 8

Corn dogs are quintessential summer fare, and these crab corn dogs are a decidedly grown-up treat for a summer party. The traditional wiener is replaced with a rich crab and shrimp sausage that's been enhanced with flavourful lobster paste made from the soft green digestive glands, essentially liver and pancreas. (It can be found at Boyd's Lobster Shop and North Sea Fish Market.) A side of wakame seaweed salad adds a sweet, briny crunch of the ocean. Use a long cutting board—at least 24 inches—for the rolling of the sausage; this will allow you to work on it lengthwise.

Corn dog dipping sauce In a medium bowl, combine all ingredients, whisking until sugar is dissolved. Store in a non-reactive container until ready to serve.

Wakame seaweed salad In a bowl, combine seaweed and tea and soak overnight in the refrigerator. Drain well, then rinse seaweed under cold running water. Squeeze out excess water and cut into matchsticks.

In a bowl, mix together seaweed, green onions and carrots and set aside. In a separate bowl, whisk together vinegar, soy sauce, sesame oil, sugar, ginger and garlic purées and chili flakes until sugar is dissolved. Pour dressing over seaweed mixture and toss to coat well. Add sesame seeds, then set aside.

Crab and shrimp sausage Process shrimp, cream and lobster paste in a food processor until smooth. Fold in crabmeat, chives and pepper. Transfer mixture to a piping bag fitted with a 1-inch tip. Lay plastic wrap over a large cutting board and pipe a 12-inch length of the sausage mixture evenly down the middle of the plastic wrap, leaving a 2-inch gap at each end of the plastic. (A large cutting board allows for enough room to work on the length

Cornmeal batter

½ cup all-purpose flour
⅓ cup yellow cornmeal
2 Tbsp granulated sugar
2½ tsp baking powder
¼ tsp baking soda
¼ tsp kosher salt
1 large egg yolk, beaten
½ cup buttermilk
Water or soda water (optional)

Assembly

Canola, grapeseed or sunflower oil,
   for deep frying
16 wooden skewers

of sausage.) Wrap one side of the plastic wrap over the sausage and roll tightly, compressing the mixture and pinching the ends as you roll. Twist the roll into 4 (3-inch) long sections. Repeat the entire process three more times to get 16 links.

Bring a large saucepan of water to a boil. Gently lower the sausages into the pan and bring the water back to a boil. Make sure the water retains a gentle boil after submerging the sausages. Simmer sausages for 6 minutes, or until cooked through. Transfer sausages to a bowl of ice water and submerge to stop the cooking process.

Cornmeal batter In a bowl, sift together flour, cornmeal, sugar, baking powder, baking soda and salt. Add egg yolk and buttermilk and mix well. (If mixture is too thick, thin it with a little water or soda water.)

Store in a large non-reactive container. The batter can keep for up to 3 days, but use it immediately for best results.

Assembly Heat oil in a deep-fryer or deep saucepan to a temperature of 345°F.

Skewer the crab sausages lengthwise. Coat the crab sausages, one at a time, in cornmeal batter. Holding the end of the skewer, carefully submerge the entire sausage in the oil and cook for 3 minutes. (If the pot isn't deep enough to completely submerge the sausages in oil, cook them for 90 seconds per side, or until crispy, golden and evenly cooked on both sides.)

Immediately transfer to a plate lined with paper towel to drain excess oil. Set aside for a minute to rest, then serve.

Cover a large platter with a bed of the wakame seaweed salad. Place crab corn dogs on top, the skewers pointing outward, and small bowls of dipping sauce on the side.

Meez Cuisine & Catering

Judy Wood

As well, the Meez team specializes in wedding menus, catered events and customized classes in their kitchen or at your home. They've even been known to cook and serve out of freight elevators. If there's propane or a plug-in, the show will go on.

Judy's love of high-quality ingredients (and a fearless use of butter) has resulted in a rich, French-influenced, elegant cuisine that's gained a dedicated following.

ABOUT THE CHEF

Judy Wood was raised in Montreal by parents who loved to entertain, and her early exposure to their informal and formal gatherings made an incredible impact on her. As an ambitious and fun-loving aspiring chef, she embarked on a trip to Paris and studied at the esteemed L'École de Cuisine La Varenne.

After earning a culinary diploma, she returned to Canada to work in venerable establishments such as Calgary's Four Seasons Hotel restaurant and Buchanan's Chop House. In 1998, she founded Savoury Cafe and Catering, and received the Global News Woman of Vision Award the following year. And for 13 years, Wood was the Saturday Chef on Global Calgary's *Saturday Morning News*. Judy Wood has also worked as a private chef for some of Calgary's most prominent citizens. In addition to running Meez, she leads culinary tours to France and Italy each year.

Meez knows how to bring people together over food and wine. Executive chef and co-owner Judy Wood was one of the first chefs to open a specialty food store, stocked with house-made, ready-to-eat foods. She wanted to see more families dining at home, despite everyone's hectic schedules. Her shop allowed people to enjoy quality food without the prep time.

Signatures include cedar-plank salmon with mahogany sauce and stuffed pork loin roast served with mashed potatoes and mushroom port sauce. Her skillfully prepared tarts—chicken and caramelized onion enveloped in the lightest of puff pastry—will have you calling back for more. Best of all, you don't even need to leave the house to enjoy it; these homey dishes can be ordered online for delivery.

Grilled vegetables

1 red bell pepper, stemmed, seeded and cut into batons

1 yellow bell pepper, stemmed, seeded and cut into batons

1 zucchini, cut into ¼-inch slices

½ bulb fennel, cored and cut into ¼-inch slices

8 oz cremini mushrooms, halved

2 Tbsp extra-virgin olive oil

½ tsp kosher salt

¼ tsp freshly ground black pepper

Three grains

¼ cup wild rice

½ cup barley

½ cup farro

Kosher salt and freshly ground black pepper, to taste

Gastrique

¼ cup honey

1 cup balsamic vinegar

Kosher salt, to taste

Three-Grain Salad with Grilled Vegetables and Trout

Serves 4 to 6

Our city may be landlocked, but we still love our fish, and dinner doesn't get more local or sustainable than when it's delicious fresh-water Alberta trout. The fish in this dish is paired with a satisfying three-grain salad, grilled seasonal vegetables and a simple sweet-and-sour sauce known as gastrique.

Grilled vegetables Preheat a grill over medium heat.

In a bowl, combine peppers, zucchini, fennel and mushrooms. Add oil, season with salt and pepper and toss.

Grill vegetables for 15 minutes, or until tender but not overcooked. Set aside to cool, then cut into bite-sized pieces.

Three grains The grains need to be cooked separately so that their flavours stay intact. Fill three saucepans with water and bring to a boil. Add wild rice, reduce heat to medium-low and simmer for 45 minutes, or until cooked through and tender. (Add more water to the pan if necessary to ensure the wild rice is always covered.) Drain and set aside.

Add barley to the second saucepan of water and cook for 30 minutes, or until tender. (Add more water to the pan if necessary to ensure the barley is always covered.) Drain and set aside.

Add farro to the third saucepan of water and cook for 30 minutes, or until tender. (Add more water to the pan if necessary to ensure the farro is always covered.) Drain and set aside.

In a large bowl, toss together grains and vegetables and mix well. Season with salt and pepper, then set aside.

Trout

Grated zest of 1 lemon

1 Tbsp grainy mustard

1 tsp honey

1 Tbsp extra-virgin olive oil,
    plus extra for brushing

1 (1¼-lb) trout fillet, skin on

Sea salt

1 tsp microgreens, for garnish

1 tsp finely sliced green onions,
    for garnish (optional)

Gastrique Heat honey in a small saucepan over medium-low and cook for 5 minutes, or until light amber in colour. Add vinegar and cook for 15 minutes, or until syrupy. Season with salt.

Trout In a small bowl, combine lemon zest, mustard, honey and oil. Spread mixture evenly over flesh side of fish. Brush the skin with oil.

Heat a large frying pan over medium-high heat. Add trout, skin side down, and season with salt. Cook for 5 minutes, or until the skin is crispy, slightly charred and blistered. Flip and cook for another 1 to 2 minutes, until cooked through. Set aside.

Assembly Toss grains and vegetables with gastrique, then transfer to a serving platter. Top with trout, garnish with microgreens and green onions, if using, and serve.

Tomato-gin jam

2 cups grape or cherry tomatoes

1 Tbsp extra-virgin olive oil

Kosher salt and freshly ground
  black pepper, to taste

¼ cup granulated sugar

½ cup red wine or sherry vinegar

¼ cup gin

Goat cheese sandwich

8 slices sourdough bread

Unsalted butter, room temperature

1 quantity Tomato-Gin Jam (see here)

1 lb Florette (goat brie), room
  temperature

Kosher salt and freshly ground black
  pepper, to taste

Tomato-Gin Jam and Grilled Goat Cheese Sandwich

Makes 4

This is a thoroughly grown-up version of a childhood favourite. The subtle tang of Florette (a brie-like goat cheese that's available at your local cheesemonger) mingles with umami-rich tomato jam in a lightly grilled and crispy sandwich. The result is a perfectly balanced dish that is truly the sum of its parts. Serve with a Belgian witbier for a simple yet satisfying meal.

Tomato-gin jam Preheat oven to 400°F. Line a baking sheet with parchment paper.

In a bowl, toss tomatoes with oil, salt and pepper. Transfer to the prepared baking sheet and roast for 10 to 15 minutes. Remove pan from oven and briefly shake it to prevent the tomatoes from sticking. Cook for another 10 minutes, until the tomato skins are brown and blistered. Remove from oven and set pan aside.

Combine sugar and ½ cup water in a saucepan and cook over medium heat until the sugar dissolves. Pour in vinegar and cook for 8 to 10 minutes, until reduced by half. Add tomatoes and gin and simmer for another 20 minutes, or until mixture is reduced and thickened like jam. Season with salt and pepper.

Goat cheese sandwich Take two slices of bread and generously butter one side of each. Place, buttered side down, on a clean work surface and spread a thick layer of tomato jam onto one slice. Top with slices of goat brie. Sprinkle with salt and pepper, then top with the other buttered slice of bread (unbuttered side down). Repeat with the remaining bread and filling.

Heat a frying pan over medium heat. Place the buttered sandwich in the pan, press down gently with a spatula and cook for 3 to 4 minutes, until bread is golden and cheese has started to melt. Flip, then cook for another 1 to 2 minutes, until bread is golden and cheese is gooey. Remove from heat and keep warm. Repeat with the remaining sandwiches.

Slice the sandwiches and enjoy!

Mercato
Spencer Wheaton

While the inimitable founder Victor has passed on, the next generation carries on his legacy. They continue to dish out top-notch Italian comfort food and make every customer feel like part of the family. And really, what more can one ask for?

ABOUT THE CHEF

Calgary's love for Mercato has never waned, and the restaurant owes much of that success to Chef Spencer Wheaton, who has been at the helm of the Mercato kitchen since 2005. His love for travelling and exposure to simple lifestyles revolving around food and family opened his eyes. "My trips to Italy always involve eating, drinking and visiting family, wineries, farms and suppliers," Wheaton tells us. "Some of my most memorable experiences have been foraging for porcini mushrooms, making wine and visiting Victor and Cathy's hometown in Calabria."

The Caracciolo family are all about food. Their first venture began in 1974, when Cathy and Victor Caracciolo founded Italian Centre in Bridgeland. In 1983, their daughter, Franca Bellusci, and her husband, Peter, opened Italian Gourmet Foods across the street. Dominic, Cathy and Victor's son, merged the two businesses, moved it to Mission in 2005 and renamed it Mercato.

The rustic ingredient-driven menu is full of southern Italian flavours. Standout Italian staples are the octopus carpaccio and the *bistecca alla fiorentina*, a classic Italian T-bone steak traditionally made with Chianina cattle—though Mercato uses AAA-grade Alberta beef, which according to Chef Spencer Wheaton is far superior.

Beans

1 cup dried cannellini or Great Northern white beans

1 clove garlic

1 bay leaf

1 Tbsp extra-virgin olive oil

Bread crumb

2 ends country-style bread, cut into large chunks

2 Tbsp olive oil

1 clove garlic, finely chopped

1 tsp kosher salt, to taste

Kale alla ribollita

3 bunches black kale, stems removed and leaves torn into chunks

1 Tbsp extra-virgin olive oil, plus extra for drizzling

¼ cup finely chopped pancetta

1 clove garlic, finely chopped

Pinch of red chili flakes

¼ cup dry white wine

½ cup canned plum tomatoes, puréed

1 cup Beans (see here)

Kosher salt, to taste

Farmhouse bread, sliced, to serve

Good-quality butter or olive oil, to serve

Serves 4 (as a side)

Tuscan Kale alla Ribollita

This dish is an adaptation of the classic Tuscan soup *ribollita*. Featuring healthy kale, hearty beans and savoury pancetta, this fortifying side is perfect for winter months. Since the beans are soaked overnight, start preparing them a day in advance.

Beans Place beans in a saucepan of cold water and soak overnight. Drain, then rinse under cold running water.

Refill the pan with fresh water and add garlic, bay leaf and oil. Bring to a boil over high heat, skimming any froth from the surface. Reduce heat to medium-low and simmer for 40 to 60 minutes, until beans are very tender. Drain, discarding the bay leaf, and set aside.

Bread crumb Preheat oven to 250°F.

Place bread on a baking sheet and bake for 30 minutes, or until bread is completely dry. Transfer bread to a food processor and pulse until finely crumbled.

Heat oil in a large frying pan over medium heat. Add half the garlic and sauté for 20 seconds. (Do not allow to burn.) Add bread crumbs and the rest of garlic and toast for 1 to 2 minutes, until brown and fragrant. Stir in salt. Set aside to cool.

Kale alla ribollita Wash kale thoroughly and set aside.

Heat oil in a large frying pan over medium heat. Add pancetta and sauté for 4 minutes, or until browned. Add garlic and chili flakes and sauté for another 3 minutes, or until fragrant. Pour in wine and deglaze the pan.

Add puréed tomatoes, beans and kale. Pour in 2 cups water and cover pan with a tight-fitting lid. Cook for 10 minutes, uncover and cook for another 5 minutes, or until kale is tender and most of the liquid has evaporated. Season with salt.

Transfer to a rustic serving vessel. Drizzle oil and sprinkle bread crumbs overtop. Serve with bread and butter (or olive oil).

▶ Pollo al Mattone with Caponata | p. 136

Spatchcock chicken

¼ cup extra-virgin olive oil,
  plus extra for greasing
3 cloves garlic
1 Tbsp fennel seeds
2 tsp red chili flakes
2 tsp kosher salt
2 tsp freshly ground black pepper
Small handful of Italian parsley
Small handful of rosemary
Small handful of sage
Small handful of thyme
1 (3-lb) whole chicken

Caponata

½ cup olive or canola oil
1 eggplant, cut into large chunks
1 cup ripened cherry tomatoes,
  quartered
¼ cup green olives, pitted and halved
2 Tbsp extra-virgin olive oil
2 Tbsp pine nuts, toasted
1 Tbsp capers, rinsed
1 clove garlic, finely chopped

Pinch of red chili flakes
1 lemon, half juiced and half cut
  into wedges
½ cup mixed herbs (such as
  Italian parsley, basil, mint and
  tarragon), roughly torn
Kosher salt and freshly ground
  black pepper, to taste

Serves 4

Pollo al Mattone with Caponata

The age-old Italian cooking technique used for this dish—*pollo al mattone*, amusingly, means "chicken under a brick"—dates back hundreds of years. The poultry would be butterflied, then weighed down with bricks or stones to help the meat cook quickly and evenly, and yield very crispy skin. The summery *caponata* is the perfect accompaniment.

Spatchcock chicken Combine all ingredients except chicken in a blender or food processor and process to a rough paste. Set aside.

Using a pair of butcher scissors, remove the chicken's backbone: Start at the thigh end and work your way up one side of the backbone. Turn chicken around, then cut along the other side. (The backbone can be reserved for stock.) Turn the bird over and cut off the wing tips. Using your palms, crack the breast bone and flatten the chicken as much as possible.

Place chicken in a casserole dish and rub herb paste all over until well coated. Cover with plastic wrap and refrigerate for 2 to 8 hours.

Remove the chicken from the refrigerator and set aside for 30 minutes to come to room temperature.

Preheat a grill to 500°F. Place a cast-iron frying pan inside the grill and close the lid. When both grill and pan are extremely hot, turn off the gas on one side, for indirect grilling. (Alternatively, if using wood or charcoal, move coals to one side.) Generously oil the grill rack and place the chicken, skin side down, on the unlit side. Lay a sheet of aluminum foil over the chicken and, using oven mitts, place the hot frying pan on top. Close the lid and cook for 25 to 30 minutes, until the thickest part of the thigh reaches an internal temperature of 165°F.

Using oven mitts, take the frying pan off the chicken. Using tongs, gently transfer the chicken by the leg to a platter without tearing the skin. Remove foil and let rest for 10 minutes.

Caponata Line a plate with paper towel and set aside.

Heat oil in a high-sided frying pan over medium heat. Working in batches, fry eggplant for 6 to 8 minutes, until golden brown. Using a slotted spoon, transfer eggplant to a plate lined with paper towel. Repeat with the remaining eggplant, making sure to bring oil back up to temperature first.

In a bowl, combine tomatoes, olives, extra-virgin olive oil, pine nuts, capers, garlic, chili flakes and lemon juice. Add eggplants and herbs and toss well. Season with salt and pepper.

Assembly Place lemon wedges on the grill and grill for 1 to 2 minutes, or until grill marks appear.

Cut chicken into quarters and arrange on a serving platter or wooden board. Spoon some caponata overtop and serve the rest on the side with the grilled lemon wedges. Serve immediately, family-style.

Pictured | p. 135

Modern Steak
Dustin Schafer

The ever-changing menu is a carnivore's paradise, but there is something for everyone. Pescatarians will appreciate wild-caught steelhead salmon served with barley risotto and brown butter, or B.C. ling cod with harissa-spiced Israeli couscous and stewed peppers. The veggie shepherd's pie is a satisfying treat for vegans.

ABOUT THE CHEF

Dustin Schafer loves cooking. After several cheffing stints in Medicine Hat and Edmonton, Schafer moved to Calgary and spent five years as executive chef of Sky 360. He was a natural fit, channelling his energy, enthusiasm and love of cooking into helping create a truly modern steakhouse that serves the best beef available.

As Modern Steak's corporate chef and resident onsite butcher, Schafer runs the kitchens for both the Kensington NW and downtown locations. While he can break down a beef carcass with the best, his passion for food extends to every aspect of the kitchen, and his high standards resonate with the rest of the team. "If you believe in what you are doing and you're working with the best ingredients, why leave?" he says.

Modern Steak has reimagined the steakhouse concept. Tucked away on a side street in Kensington, this bright and open restaurant has a monochromatic scheme, a private back room and a downstairs bar. (It even has sound-absorbing panels to improve acoustics!)

Modern Steak knows quality and guarantees some of the best steak in the province. It teamed up with Benchmark Angus to purchase an award-winning black Angus bull (named Premium), famed for siring calves that have Prime marbled meat. The restaurant also serves Brant Lake wagyu, grass-fed beef from Pine Haven Ranch and Springbank Ranch elk and bison.

Granola
½ cup old-fashioned oats
¼ cup almonds
¼ cup pecans
¼ cup sunflower seeds
1 Tbsp maple syrup
1 Tbsp olive or grapeseed oil
½ tsp sea salt, or to taste

Roasted carrots
1 bunch baby carrots
    (about 1 lb), peeled
1 Tbsp olive or canola oil
Sea salt to taste

Maple mascarpone
½ cup mascarpone
2 Tbsp whipping cream or
    crème fraîche
1 Tbsp maple syrup

Roasted Carrots with Granola and Maple Mascarpone

Serves 2

Creamy, crunchy, sweet and savoury, this dish hits all the right notes in flavours and textures. You can easily double the yummy granola recipe to have it on hand.

Granola Preheat oven to 350°F. Line a baking sheet with parchment paper.

In a bowl, combine all ingredients. Spread mixture on the prepared baking sheet in a single layer. Bake for 15 to 20 minutes, until golden brown.

Roasted carrots Preheat oven to 350°F. Line a baking sheet with parchment paper.

In a bowl, toss together all ingredients. Transfer to the prepared baking sheet and roast for 30 minutes, or until carrots are tender, with a touch of colour.

Maple mascarpone In a mixer fitted with the paddle attachment, combine all ingredients, whipping at maximum speed for 1 minute, or until creamy and loose. (Do not overmix or mascarpone will curdle.)

Assembly Place carrots on a serving platter, spoon maple mascarpone overtop and sprinkle with granola. Serve family-style.

Pictured | p. 140

Peppercorn sauce

3 Tbsp unsalted butter

1 Tbsp finely chopped shallots

2 cloves garlic, chopped

3½ Tbsp canned green peppercorns, drained (divided)

2 Tbsp brandy

1 Tbsp all-purpose flour

2 cups beef stock, plus extra as needed

Kosher salt, to taste

2 Tbsp whipping cream

Steak

2 (10-oz) rib-eye or sirloin steaks, 1 to 1½ inches thick

Canola oil, for brushing

4 tsp kosher salt, plus extra to taste

Freshly ground black pepper, to taste

NOTE: Do not pepper the steak at the start of the cooking process. If you choose to, do so only at the end of the cooking time, otherwise the pepper will burn on the grill and add bitterness to the steak. You can also brush the cooked steak with garlic oil. In a small frying pan, heat 1 cup olive oil and a handful of garlic cloves (no need to peel) over low heat for 1 hour, or until oil has the strong, alluring scent of garlic. Moderate the heat so the garlic doesn't brown. Remove from heat, cool and strain. Oil can be stored in the refrigerator for up to 1 month.

Serves 2

Steak with Peppercorn Sauce

Alberta has some of the finest beef in the world, reflecting our quality pastures, grain and animal husbandries. For this recipe, consider splurging on high-quality meat from a trusted butcher—you don't need to do much to it to coax out flavour, and this classic with peppercorn sauce takes it right over the top.

Peppercorn sauce Melt butter in a large saucepan over medium heat. Add shallots and sauté for 1 minute. Reduce heat to low, add garlic and cook for 2 minutes until shallots are translucent and garlic is fragrant. Place half of the peppercorns on a cutting board and, using the side of a knife, crush them. Add crushed and whole peppercorns to the pan.

Add brandy and cook for another 5 minutes, or until liquid is reduced by half. Stir in flour until a paste forms and cook for 1 minute, or until nutty and golden brown. Pour in stock, a third at a time, whisking continuously. Reduce heat to medium-low and simmer for 15 to 20 minutes. Season with salt.

Remove from heat and set aside for 30 minutes. Stir in cream, bring to a simmer and remove from heat. If the sauce is too thick, thin it out with stock. If it is too thin, continue to reduce the sauce.

Steak Preheat a grill to high heat.

Bring steak to room temperature for at least 20 minutes and up to 1 hour. (This is known as tempering the steak.) Brush oil over steaks and generously season with salt.

Place steaks on the grill at an angle and leave for 3 minutes. Rotate steak 90 degrees and leave for another 3 minutes. Flip steak and repeat rotation to create a criss-cross pattern. (Try to use a different spot on the barbecue when flipping the steak to get maximum heat.)

Remove steak from the grill and let rest for 10 minutes. Keep the grill hot.

Assembly Quickly reheat steaks by placing them on the grill for 30 seconds on each side. Transfer to a serving platter, brush with oil and sprinkle with salt and pepper. Pour over a generous amount of peppercorn sauce. Serve immediately.

Native Tongues Taqueria
Rodrigo Rodas

"Native Tongues is a fully encompassing Mexican dining experience," co-owner Willis explains. "It's like being in a funky cantina in the heart of Mexico City. When diners step into the space, we want their worries of the day to melt away."

ABOUT THE CHEF

Executive chef Rodrigo Rodas's esteemed career began when he was 18. After attending a culinary program in Mexico City, Rodas interned at the Restaurant Mandarine in Monte Carlo, Monaco. From there he went on to work at Au Pied de Cochon in Mexico City and at the Four Seasons Punta Mita. Born and raised in Mexico City, Rodas's passion for cooking is rooted in Central Mexico's cuisine. And much to our delight, he has brought his knowledge to Calgary.

"The dishes I create for Native Tongues are based on tradition and preserve the authentic flavours of Mexico," he tells us. "I consider myself an ambassador of Mexico and try to represent the country as best as I can."

You cannot go wrong with authentic Mexican food, and nobody in Calgary knows this better than Chef Cody Willis. When he opened a taco pop-up called Taco or No Taco, he amassed a strong and loyal following. So it came as no surprise that Native Tongues Taqueria was an immediate success upon opening.

Located in Victoria Park, the restaurant is adorned with iconic Mexican paintings, prints and artifacts. In the open kitchen, a wood-burning grill takes centre stage, while an extended bar serves refreshing libations fuelled with mezcal. When you're wanting a casual and fuss-free evening with friends and family, you can trust Native Tongues to deliver simple ingredients and bold flavours for classic Mexican food.

Nopales salad

6 fresh or jarred nopales

3 Roma tomatoes, thinly sliced

1 small white onion, thinly sliced

2 small serrano peppers, stemmed, seeded and finely chopped

Bunch of cilantro, finely chopped

2 Tbsp finely chopped oregano

2 Tbsp kosher salt, plus extra to taste

½ cup extra-virgin olive oil

Juice of 3 limes

Assembly

25 (4-inch) corn tortillas (preferably tortillas taqueras)

3 large ripe avocados

1 lime

Kosher salt, to taste

1 cup grated queso fresco

Serves 6 to 8

Nopales Salad Tacos

Nopales, or nopal pads, are the edible leaves of the prickly pear cactus, often used for a salad. Tart, citrusy, high in fibre and rich in pectin, they are like a combination of rhubarb and aloe vera. It's believed that, in addition to lowering cholesterol, nopales can cure a hangover (if consumed *before* drinking). Now that's the kind of cactus we can all appreciate!

Nopales salad When using fresh nopales, the spines must first be removed. Wearing gloves, hold a pad by its stem end and trim off the edges. Run a potato peeler along the surface of the nopales to remove the thorns. Repeat with the other side.

Thinly slice the nopales, then soak them in a bowl of cold water for 10 minutes to remove the natural slime from the cactus. Drain, fill bowl with more cold water and soak for another 10 minutes. Repeat one more time for a total soaking time of 30 minutes.

Meanwhile, in a separate bowl, combine the remaining ingredients, stirring to mix well. Cover and reserve in the refrigerator.

Fill a bowl with ice water. Bring a large saucepan of salted water to a boil. Add drained nopales to the pan. Reduce heat to medium-low and gently simmer for 2 minutes, or until nopales turn bright green. Drain, then transfer them to the ice bath to cool. Drain again.

Take tomato mixture out of the refrigerator. Add nopales and stir, adjusting salt to taste. Cover and refrigerate until needed.

The salad can be stored in the refrigerator for up to 2 days.

Assembly Line a large dinner plate with a clean dish towel.

Heat a cast-iron frying pan over high heat. Add a tortilla and warm on both sides. Transfer to the prepared plate and cover with a dish towel to keep warm. Repeat with the remaining tortillas.

Slice avocados, then squeeze lime juice overtop and season with salt. This keeps the avocado from browning.

Top each tortilla with nopales salad, a teaspoon of queso fresco and a slice of avocado. Wash down with ice-cold beer.

Pictured | p. 145

▶ Nopales Salad Tacos | p. 143
Marinated BBQ Chicken | p. 146

Adobo sauce

½ cup canola oil

7 ancho chilies, seeded, stemmed and broken into pieces

7 guajillo chilies, seeded, stemmed and broken into pieces

4 large avocado leaves

6 cloves garlic

2 Tbsp white wine vinegar

1 tsp ground cinnamon

1 tsp ground cumin

1 tsp dried oregano

½ tsp ground allspice

Kosher salt, to taste

Pollo adobado

1 to 2 banana leaves

2 white onions, thinly sliced

2 carrots, thinly sliced

2 (5-lb) whole chickens

Kosher salt, to taste

2 cups Adobo Sauce (see here)

Pickled onions and peppers

½ cup apple cider vinegar

1 tsp kosher salt

1 red onion, thinly sliced

2 serrano peppers, stemmed, seeded and thinly sliced

Assembly

1 bunch cilantro, coarsely chopped

Thinly sliced onions, for garnish

Lime wedges, for garnish

Salsa, for garnish

Nopales Salad (p. 143), for garnish

50 tortillas taqueras or 30 (6-inch) corn tortillas, to serve

Serves 8 to 10

Marinated BBQ Chicken

Known in Spanish as *pollo adobado a la barbacoa*, this party dish serves up a whole lot of chicken, which is perfect for tacos. Take care to not inhale the fumes of the dried peppers as they fry. Wrapping the chicken in banana leaves is an essential part of the flavour of this dish, but in a pinch, it can be wrapped in parchment paper. Banana and avocado leaves can be found at your local Unimarket or La Tiendona.

Adobo sauce Heat oil in a frying pan over medium heat. Add chilies and sauté for 2 minutes, or until they turn a deeper red. Stand back to avoid inhaling the fumes, which can induce a coughing attack. Remove pan from heat and set aside to cool. Strain oil and reserve for later.

Put chilies in a food processor or blender, add the remaining ingredients except salt and purée to a thick paste. (Add warm water to loosen, if needed.)

Heat reserved chili oil in a saucepan over low heat. Stir in the chili paste and fry mixture for 10 minutes, scraping the bottom of the pan frequently to release any browned bits. Season with salt. Set aside to cool, then transfer to a container and refrigerate until needed. (It will keep in the refrigerator for up to 2 weeks.)

Pollo adobado Preheat oven to 350°F.

Arrange banana leaves (or parchment paper) along the bottom and sides of a large ovenproof dish (such as a turkey roaster or a 10-litre casserole dish), leaving enough of the leaves around the edges to fold over and cover the top of the adobo. Scatter onions and carrots into the dish.

Cut each chicken into 4 pieces, bones-in: 2 legs or thighs and 2 breasts with wings attached. Place chicken on top of vegetables and season with salt. Pour adobo sauce over chicken pieces, ensuring they are thoroughly covered. Fold edges of banana leaves overtop and put a lid on the casserole dish.

Bake for 45 minutes, or until chicken is juicy and liquid runs clear, or until the thickest part of chicken reaches an internal temperature of 165°F.

Pickled onions and peppers In a small bowl, combine vinegar, salt and ½ cup water, stirring to mix well. Add onion and peppers, then set aside for 10 minutes.

Assembly When the chicken is cooked, let rest for 2 to 3 minutes, then transfer to a large serving platter and pour the leftover juice from the casserole dish overtop.

Drain pickled onion mixture, discarding the liquid or saving it for another pickling session. The chicken is pulled from the bones by each guest as they build their tacos. Garnish with cilantro, sliced onions, lime wedges, salsa and the nopales salad (p. 143). Serve with tortillas.

Our Daily Brett
Brett McDermott

Good, honest food. These three words neatly encapsulate the philosophy behind Our Daily Brett (or "ODB," as regulars call it). ODB is a boutique market and catering company located in Calgary's Marda Loop neighbourhood. The market features a carefully curated selection of culinary and lifestyle products and an always-changing menu of grab-and-go foods. A long harvest table sits in the centre of the market for customers to linger around while enjoying a snack or beverage from the ODB café menu. In 2017, ODB opened a sister café in Altadore called Neighbour Coffee and also launched Salon Fine Catering & Events to formalize its full-service catering and events offerings.

ABOUT THE CHEF

Brett McDermott has learned to do by doing. His mom used to put him to work in her kitchen to keep him out of trouble. (Interesting side note: McDermott's mom lives in the former home of Helen Miles, co-author of the legendary Best of Bridge cookbooks.)

In 2008, McDermott earned a bachelor of commerce degree from St. Mary's University in Halifax, Nova Scotia. While in Halifax, he was engaged in a few side hustles, including throwing a monthly art party, the format of which combined an art show with DJs from both near and far. Before opening his market, McDermott worked as a caterer and private chef, travelling to places like Maui, Belize and Nicaragua, cooking at yoga retreats and surf hotels. He also ran a meal-delivery program and worked on an organic farm in upcountry Maui. His travel and experiences culminated in opening Our Daily Brett, a community-oriented market and café that features an exciting menu inspired by McDermott's travels and offers both a wine program and catering services.

Korean steak tartare
4 oz good-quality beef flank steak

Garlic chips
¼ cup canola oil, for frying
1 head garlic, cloves separated, peeled and thinly sliced

Assembly
¼ cup kimchi
1 egg yolk
1 tsp Dijon mustard
1 tsp toasted sesame oil
1 tsp tamari
2 green onions, thinly sliced
Kosher salt and freshly ground black pepper, to taste
Kewpie mayonnaise, for garnish
8 perilla leaves, to serve

Serves 2

Korean Steak Tartare

This savoury, umami bomb is ideal for an intimate dinner or as a canapé at a cocktail party. Kimchi, Kewpie (a brand of Japanese mayonnaise) and the perilla leaves can be found at Asian grocery stores.

Korean steak tartare Using a sharp knife, finely chop flank steak until it resembles thick ground beef. Place in a metal bowl and nest inside another bowl filled with ice.

Garlic chips Line a plate with paper towel. Heat oil in a small frying pan over high heat. Add garlic, reduce heat to medium-high and sauté for 1 minute, or until browned but not burnt. Using a slotted spoon, transfer garlic to the prepared plate.

Assembly Chop kimchi slightly larger than the beef and add to the bowl of beef. Add egg yolk, Dijon, sesame oil, tamari and green onions. Mix together and season with salt and pepper.

Arrange a scoop of steak tartare on each individual plate. Garnish with a few dots of Kewpie mayonnaise, top with the fried garlic chips and serve with perilla leaves. Spoon the tartare into the leaf and pop it into your mouth.

Green goddess dressing

¾ cup aioli

¼ cup yogurt

1 Tbsp white wine vinegar

1½ Tbsp chopped green onions

1 Tbsp chopped Italian parsley

1 Tbsp chopped basil

Cayenne pepper, to taste

Kosher salt, to taste

Buckwheat groats

2 Tbsp buckwheat groats

Roasted root vegetables

8 baby carrots

8 baby beets

8 small Hakurei turnips

Canola oil, for brushing

Kosher salt and freshly ground
    black pepper, to taste

Maldon salt, for garnish

Grated zest of 1 orange, for garnish

3 Tbsp microgreens or Italian
    parsley, for garnish

2 Tbsp smoked or regular
    extra-virgin olive oil

Roasted Root Vegetables with Green Goddess and Buckwheat

Serves 4

The bright colours and flavours of this dish make it a beautiful and hearty addition to any meal. Hakurei turnips, also known as Tokyo turnips, can be found at farmers' markets around town.

Green goddess dressing Place all ingredients except cayenne and salt in a blender and blend until smooth. Season with cayenne and salt. Refrigerate until needed. The dressing can be stored in the refrigerator for up to 3 weeks.

Buckwheat groats Heat a frying pan over medium-high heat. Add buckwheat groats and toast, shaking the pan occasionally, for 4 minutes, or until fragrant and browned. Transfer to a plate and set aside until needed.

Roasted root vegetables Preheat oven to 400°F. Line a baking sheet with parchment paper.

To avoid staining the vegetables, toss each vegetable separately with oil, kosher salt and pepper. Arrange vegetables separately on the prepared baking sheet and roast for 10 to 15 minutes, until fork tender.

Assembly Spread a layer of the dressing on the bottom of a serving platter and arrange vegetables on top. Use as much dressing as you like; any extra can be saved for other uses.

Finish with Maldon salt, orange zest, microgreens (or parsley) and toasted buckwheat. Drizzle olive oil overtop and serve family-style.

Oxbow
Quinn Staple

favourites like the rib-eye burger and handmade pastas sate, comfort and leave you content all at once.

ABOUT THE CHEF

Executive chef Quinn Staple is at the helm of Oxbow, Yellow Door Bistro (p. 216) and Raw Bar (p. 158) for Hotel Arts Group, as well as of the group's extensive onsite and offsite catering options. While conceding that our climate is not ideal for a lengthy growing season, Staple marvels at the consistency of product that he sources from inventive and resourceful purveyors throughout Alberta and B.C.

Active on the local scene for chef collaborative events, Staple participated at Pig and Pinot Festival (2014–18), Alberta Open Farm Days (2015), Brewery and the Beast (2015–18), REAP's Food for Thought (2015–17) and other events with Alberta Culinary Tourism Alliance and the Hotel Arts Group to help raise the profile of local producers while highlighting their products in delicious and innovative ways. He also represented Yellow Door Bistro at the Gold Medal Plates competition in Calgary in November 2017. "I love this industry, it's ever-changing, there's so much to learn. The Calgary culinary scene and community has really grown. The food industry has given me so many opportunities, travel, and lasting friendships."

The elegant Hotel Arts Kensington is home to Oxbow, sister restaurant of Yellow Door Bistro (p. 216) and Raw Bar (p. 158). The environment, with its dark walls, blonde wood floors and tufted banquettes, is elegant yet cozy and perfectly suited for watching the latest match while enjoying a pint of Oxbow Kolsch.

More importantly, it's a restaurant where you can indulge in seasonal cuisine, thanks to the skillfully prepared and delicious food. The menus—breakfast, lunch, dinner and weekend brunch—are informal and approachable. For instance, the uncomplicated dinner menu offers shareable appetizers such as Alberta goat cheese artichoke dip, and duck wings with fermented Fresno chili sauce. And crowd

▷ Oxbow Apple Cinnamon Buns | p. 154

Cinnamon bun dough

2 tsp dry active yeast

¼ cup lukewarm (105°F to 110°F) water

4 eggs, room temperature

1 cup all-purpose flour, plus extra for dusting

1 cup pastry flour

¼ cup granulated sugar

1 Tbsp ground cinnamon

1 Tbsp sea salt

1 cup (2 sticks) unsalted butter, chilled, cubed and then left to warm to room temperature, plus extra for greasing

Apple filling

½ cup packed brown sugar

⅓ cup (⅔ stick) unsalted butter

1 tsp ground cinnamon

2 Granny Smith apples, peeled and cut into ¼-inch cubes

Streusel

¼ cup all-purpose flour

3 Tbsp granulated sugar

1 Tbsp brown sugar

1 tsp ground cinnamon

Pinch of salt

3 Tbsp unsalted butter

Bourbon caramel sauce

½ cup granulated sugar

1 tsp freshly squeezed lemon juice

½ cup whipping cream

1 Tbsp bourbon

1 Tbsp unsalted butter

Assembly

All-purpose flour, for dusting

1 Tbsp butter, melted, plus extra for greasing

Oxbow Apple Cinnamon Buns

Serves 6

For Oxbow's signature breakfast dish, six small cinnamon buns are squeezed into one baking dish, making sharing fun. Serve warm with a hit of hot bourbon caramel poured overtop.

Cinnamon bun dough In a small bowl, combine yeast and lukewarm water and set aside to rest for 10 minutes.

In a stand mixer fitted with the dough hook, combine the yeast mixture and eggs, beating for 1 minute.

In another bowl, combine both flours, sugar, cinnamon and salt. Add to the stand mixer and mix for 5 minutes on medium speed, occasionally scraping down the sides of the bowl. Reduce speed to low and mix for 1 minute.

Add ¼ cup (½ stick) butter and beat for 1 minute. Repeat three more times with the remaining butter, then beat for 10 minutes on medium speed.

Grease and lightly flour a large bowl. Place dough in bowl, cover with plastic wrap and set aside in a warm place for 3 hours, or until doubled in size.

Apple filling In a bowl, combine sugar, butter and cinnamon. Add apples and toss.

Streusel In a small bowl, combine all ingredients except butter. Using your fingers, cut in butter until mixture is coarse and crumbly. Refrigerate until needed.

Bourbon caramel sauce In a small saucepan, combine sugar and ½ cup water. (Don't get any sugar on the sides of the pot above the water.) Bring mixture to a boil, then add lemon juice. (Don't stir, as it can cause the sugar to seize or clump and burn.) Cook for 4 minutes, or until mixture turns a dark golden colour.

NOTE: Any unbaked rolls can be tightly wrapped in plastic wrap and frozen for up to 1 month. To bake, pack the frozen rolls into a greased baking dish and set aside for 3 to 4 hours, until doubled in size. Bake as directed in the recipe.

Remove pan from heat. Carefully pour in cream and bourbon (they will splatter and spit) and whisk. Stir in butter and warm through over medium heat. Remove from heat and set aside.

Assembly Preheat oven to 350°F. Grease a 9-inch square cake pan.

Turn dough onto a floured work surface and roll into a rectangle ½ inch thick. Brush dough with butter and liberally scatter apple filling on top. Cut dough in half lengthwise.

Roll dough up lengthwise into a tight cylinder, 1½ to 2 inches wide. Using a sharp knife, cut the log into 1-inch-thick rolls. Loosely pack the rolls, face side up, into the prepared baking dish. Cover with plastic wrap and set aside for 1 hour, or until doubled in size.

Sprinkle streusel overtop and bake for 20 minutes, or until golden brown. Set aside for 10 minutes, then pour over bourbon caramel sauce and serve.

Chamomile duck
1 Tbsp dried chamomile leaves
2 tsp kosher salt
Grated zest of 1 lemon
2 duck breasts, trimmed and scored

Chamomile honey
1 cup honey
1 tsp dried chamomile leaves

Assembly
1 Tbsp extra-virgin olive oil
2 Tbsp Chamomile Honey (see here)
2 Tbsp cold unsalted butter (divided)
2 cups fresh or frozen English peas

Chamomile Duck with English Peas

Serves 4

While this dish may appear to be better suited to a formal environment with white-clothed tables, monogrammed napkins and you in your Sunday best, it's really the type of standout dish you'll want to serve at any dinner party. The tangy chamomile brine complements and balances the strong flavour of the duck breast.

Chamomile duck In a saucepan, combine chamomile, salt, lemon zest and 2 cups water. Bring to a boil, then remove from heat and set aside to cool. Refrigerate until cold.

Transfer mixture to a bowl, add duck breast and brine for 2 hours at room temperature.

Remove duck from the brine and thoroughly pat dry. Reserve in the refrigerator until needed.

Chamomile honey In a small saucepan, combine honey and chamomile and warm over medium heat for 10 minutes. Remove from heat and set aside to cool to room temperature. Reserve until needed.

Assembly Heat oil in a large frying pan over medium heat. Add duck breasts, skin side down, and cook for 3 minutes. Flip and cook for another 30 seconds.

Flip over again so the skin side is down and render for 5 minutes, or until skin is golden. Drain excess fat and reserve it for future use (such as roasting potatoes).

Add the 2 tablespoons chamomile honey to the pan and bring to a boil. Add 1 tablespoon butter, then flip the duck breasts and baste with honey-butter mixture. Transfer duck to a plate, skin side up. (This keeps the skin crispy.) Reserve the honey-butter mixture.

Bring a saucepan of water to a boil, then reduce heat to medium. Add peas and cook for 5 minutes, or until peas are bright green. Drain, then return to the saucepan. Stir in the remaining 1 tablespoon butter.

Divide peas among four plates. Thinly slice duck breasts and fan out some slices on each plate. Spoon the reserved honey-butter mixture overtop and serve immediately.

Raw Bar
Quinn Staple
and Peter Paiva

And who can resist a good Happy Hour? Half-price small plates and well-priced wines, beers and cocktails lure in post-work crowds looking to relax and imbibe.

ABOUT THE CHEFS

When chef de cuisine Peter Paiva (pictured) took time off from pursuing his education degree at the University of Calgary to take a few professional cooking courses at SAIT (Southern Alberta Institute of Technology), he had no idea the sabbatical would reveal his passion and talent for cooking. India-born and Newfound-land-raised Paiva moved to Calgary to pursue a career as a chef, eventually working as a cook at Chef's Table (now known as Oxbow, p. 152) at the luxurious Kensington Riverside Inn (now Hotel Arts Kensington).

In 2017, under his helm, the Raw Bar team won the Consumers' Choice Award at the Chef Meets BC Grape event and the following year, they won the coveted Best Food and Wine Pairing award. When not in the kitchen, Paiva can be found travelling with his wife and daughter, experiencing new cultures and cuisines.

For executive chef Quinn Staple, see Oxbow (p. 152).

Raw Bar is not your run-of-the-mill craft cocktail lounge. The modern lounge, located on the main floor of Hotel Arts, is a popular pit stop among local artists, dancers and theatre patrons before they head down the street to the new Decidedly Jazz Danceworks performance space.

Sit at the bar under a glass bubble chandelier and watch expert mixologists whip up inventive drinks such as the signature Derelict (spiced plum and clove jelly, vodka and lychee liqueur) and El Mezclado (mezcal, calvados, ume plum wine and Ancho Reyes). And on a summer day, lounge at a poolside table and enjoy fresh, contemporary Asian food made with ethically sourced seafood. The menu is ever-changing, but reliable favourites such as the Thai curry noodle bowl are always hit the spot.

Beef and kimchi dumplings

3 Tbsp kosher salt (divided)

¾ cup sweet potato noodles

2 lbs beef chuck flats, chopped, or ground beef

8 oz tiger prawns, peeled, deveined and finely chopped

5 Tbsp finely chopped ginger

1 cup finely chopped kimchi

¼ cup finely chopped green onions, white part only

1 Tbsp fish sauce

1 tsp granulated sugar

2 large eggs, beaten

1 Tbsp freshly ground black pepper

20 round dumpling wrappers

Ssamjang dipping sauce

2 Tbsp sesame oil

2 shallots, coarsely chopped

6 cloves garlic, chopped

¼ cup chopped green onions

2 Tbsp sesame seeds

¾ cup doenjang (fermented Korean bean paste)

¼ cup gochujang (fermented Korean chili paste)

¼ cup honey

1 Tbsp cayenne pepper

Juice of 1 lime

Assembly

Canola oil, for frying

Ito togarashi (strands of dried chili), for garnish

Pickled vegetables, for garnish

Chopped green onions, for garnish

Black and white sesame seeds, for garnish

Beef and Kimchi Dumplings with Ssamjang Dipping Sauce

Makes 20 dumplings

These popular dumplings are easy to make and great for sharing. This recipe calls for beef chuck, but ground beef is a good substitute. Ssamjang, a delicious spicy dipping sauce, is made with *doenjang* (fermented bean paste) and *gochujang* (fermented chili paste) both of which can be purchased at Asian grocery stores, including Arirang Oriental Foods and T&T. The dumplings freeze well, so make a large batch and cook them from frozen when you wish.

Beef and kimchi dumplings In a saucepan, bring 3 cups water and 1 tablespoon salt to a boil over high heat. Add noodles and cook for 5 minutes, or until translucent and softened. Fill a bowl with ice water. Drain noodles, then put them in the bowl of ice water to cool. Drain and chop into ½-inch pieces. Cover and set aside.

In a large bowl, combine beef, prawns and ginger and, using your hands, mix well. Set aside.

In a separate bowl, combine kimchi, green onion, fish sauce and sugar. Add eggs, beef mixture, noodles, the remaining 2 tablespoons salt and pepper. Using your hands, mix thoroughly.

Line one or two baking sheets with waxed paper. Take a dumpling wrapper and spoon a tablespoon of the filling into the centre. Fill a small bowl with water. Using a brush or your fingertip, wet the edge of the wrapper. Fold over half the dumpling wrapper to form a half-moon shape, then press to seal edges together. Place on the prepared baking sheet, and repeat until all the dumplings have been made.

NOTE: To freeze the dumplings, place the sheet(s) of prepared dumplings in the freezer. Once frozen, transfer to a freezer bag. When ready to serve, generously sprinkle a layer of flour on a baking sheet, add the frozen dumplings in a single layer and thaw. (If you leave the dumplings in the bag to thaw, they will stick together.)

Ssamjang dipping sauce Heat oil in a small frying pan over medium-high heat. Add shallots, reduce heat to medium and sauté for 5 minutes, or until softened. Add garlic and cook, covered, for 5 minutes. Uncover and sauté until slightly browned.

Transfer mixture to a food processor, add green onions and sesame seeds and pulse until mixed through but still chunky. Set aside to cool completely.

In a separate bowl, combine doenjang, gochujang, honey, cayenne and lime juice. Fold in onion-sesame mixture. (Sauce can be stored in an airtight container in the refrigerator for up to 4 weeks.)

Assembly Heat 1 tablespoon oil in a non-stick frying pan over high heat. Working in batches, add 8 to 10 dumplings and sear for 4 to 5 minutes, until browned. Flip, add ¼ cup water and cover pan. Reduce heat to medium and cook for another 4 to 5 minutes, until water has completely evaporated. Transfer dumplings to a serving platter and repeat with remaining dumplings.

Garnish with ito togarashi, pickled vegetables, green onions, and sesame seeds. Serve with a side of ssamjang sauce for dipping.

Plum and clove jelly
¾ cup canned plums
¼ cup raw sugar
2 Tbsp finely chopped ginger
2 whole cloves
½ cinnamon stick

Derelict cocktail
½ fl oz vodka
½ fl oz Soho lychee liqueur
½ fl oz Plum and Clove Jelly (see here),
    plus extra for garnish
1 fl oz pineapple juice
1 fl oz freshly squeezed lemon juice
Granulated sugar, to rim glass
Edible flowers, for garnish (optional)

Serves 1

Derelict Cocktail

The award-winning Derelict has been a signature cocktail at Raw Bar since 2005. It has a double dose of plum and clove jelly—within the drink and as the garnish.

Plum and clove jelly In a small saucepan, combine all ingredients and bring to a boil. Reduce heat to medium-low and simmer for 5 minutes. Strain jelly into a small bowl, pressing through as much pulp as possible. Chill and reserve.

Derelict cocktail In a martini shaker, combine vodka, lychee liqueur, jelly, pineapple juice and lemon juice. Add a scoop of ice and shake vigorously for 1 minute.

Assembly Fill a saucer with water. Have another saucer of sugar ready. Dip the rim of a martini glass or your favourite coupe glass into the water, then dip into sugar.

   Strain the cocktail into the sugared martini glass and garnish with a small scoop of plum and clove jelly and edible flowers, if using.

River Café
Matthias Fong

Saskatoon berries and puffed red fife, and juniper-smoked goose served alongside grilled corn polenta, lobster mushrooms and birch syrup. It comes as no surprise that the restaurant constantly ranks on Canada's 100 Best Restaurants list (2015, 2016, 2017, 2018) and *Avenue* magazine's Calgary's 25 Best Restaurants list, and won Best of Award of Excellence from Wine Spectator multiple times, just to name a few!

River Café, as well as its sister restaurant, Deane House (p. 82), continues to lead and evolve with sustainability initiatives, including an edible garden and green-energy power.

ABOUT THE CHEF

Executive chef Matthias Fong oversees two of the best kitchens in Calgary: those of Deane House and River Café. He worked at Michelin-starred Marcus (a Marcus Wareing restaurant), which specializes in contemporary British seasonal cuisine, and discovered the potential for developing a Canadian cuisine. When Fong returned to Calgary, he began to explore local and regional ingredients, especially those from the gardens surrounding the restaurant. "My hope has been to develop a distinctly contemporary Canadian cuisine through ingredients, history and culture," he says.

Fong's completely Canadian menu received University of Guelph's Good Food Innovation Award in 2017 and earned him a silver medal at Gold Medal Plates.

During the short walk over the Bow River and into the park to River Café, something magical happens: the city seems to disappear. Founder Sal Howell transformed an open-air concession stand into an exceptional restaurant by repurposing found materials and working with local artists. A boat was transformed into a bar, a fieldstone fireplace was built, and an oven and grill in the open kitchen was fuelled by orchard wood. It was an immediate success.

And from the outset, River Café has committed to regional cuisine made with local, wild-foraged and heirloom ingredients. (In fact, the restaurant's pantry is stocked with dried herbs and spices harvested the previous year from its garden.) This is where you'll find red lentil hummus served with Highwood Crossing flatbread, bison tartare elevated by wild garlic,

▶ Winter Squash and Mushroom Tart | p. 166

Tart shell

3 cups + 1 Tbsp all-purpose flour, plus extra for dusting

1 cup buckwheat flour

2 tsp salt (preferably Vancouver Island salt)

2 cups (4 sticks) cold unsalted butter, diced into 1-inch cubes

1 large egg, beaten

Custard

4 large eggs

1 cup heavy cream

1 cup whole milk

1 tsp kosher salt

Filling

4 cups oyster mushrooms, cut into bite-sized pieces

Kosher salt and freshly ground black pepper, to taste

1 small winter squash (such as butternut, acorn, spaghetti, red kuri or delicata), peeled, seeded and cut into 1-inch cubes

2 Tbsp canola oil

½ cup (1 stick) unsalted butter

1 leek, white and light green parts only, halved lengthwise and cut into 1-inch pieces

1 small yellow onion, thinly sliced

1 small red onion, thinly sliced

1 small shallot, thinly sliced

1 Tbsp garlic, chopped

1 cup shredded aged Gouda (preferably Vital Greens) or goat feta (preferably Fairwinds Farm)

Assembly

Fresh greens, to serve

3 Tbsp goat yogurt (preferably Fairwinds Farm), to serve

Winter Squash and Mushroom Tart

Serves 10

Whether it's for a lazy brunch, a summer evening dinner or a comforting winter meal to stave off the darkness and cold, it's hard to go wrong with a rich and satisfying savoury tart. Especially when it's paired with a crisp green salad and an amber beer or glass of full-bodied red wine.

Tart shell In a stand mixer fitted with the paddle attachment, combine both flours, salt and butter and mix until pea-sized lumps form. Gradually add ½ cup cold water, a little at a time, until the dough comes together. Do not overmix. Wrap dough in plastic wrap and refrigerate for at least 30 minutes and up to overnight.

Preheat oven to 350°F. Place the oven rack in the centre. Line a 12- × 18-inch baking sheet with parchment paper.

On a lightly floured work surface, roll out dough to a 14- × 20-inch rectangle. Lay it on the prepared baking sheet, leaving a 1-inch overhang of dough on each side. Lay a second piece of parchment paper on top of the dough and cover with baking beans. Refrigerate for 5 minutes.

Bake for 20 minutes, or until edges are golden and the bottom of the pastry is cooked through. Remove baking beans and brush the tart shell with egg. Bake for another 10 minutes, or until tart shell is golden. Set aside to cool to room temperature.

Custard In a blender, purée all ingredients until well mixed. Pass through a fine-mesh sieve and set aside.

Filling Line a 12- × 18-inch baking sheet with parchment paper.

Place mushrooms on the prepared baking sheet and bake for 10 minutes, or until golden and slightly dehydrated. Transfer into a bowl and season with salt and pepper.

In a large bowl, toss squash with oil, salt and pepper. Roast for 30 minutes, or until squash is tender and lightly caramelized. Set aside.

Meanwhile, heat butter in a large frying pan over medium heat. Add leek, yellow and red onions, shallot and garlic and sauté for 8 to 10 minutes, until onions are softened and translucent. Add mushrooms and squash, stirring to mix well, and sauté until heated through. Remove from heat.

Assembly Spread filling evenly on top of pastry. Bake for 5 minutes. Remove from oven and spread the custard overtop. Sprinkle with cheese. Bake for 15 to 20 minutes, until custard is set and cheese is golden. Set tart aside to cool for 5 to 10 minutes.

Cut it into 10 pieces and serve with fresh greens and spoonfuls of yogurt.

Pictured | p. 165

Roasted garlic
1 head garlic
Canola oil, for drizzling

Red lentil hummus
2 cups dried red lentils
¼ cup dry white wine
3 cloves garlic
4 cloves Roasted Garlic (see here)
3 Roma tomatoes, halved
⅔ cup canola oil (preferably Highwood Crossing)
¼ cup coriander seeds, toasted and finely ground

2 Tbsp apple cider vinegar
2 tsp kosher salt, or to taste
¼ tsp chipotle powder
1 tsp sumac
Favourite pickled vegetables, chips, crudité, bread or crackers, to serve

Serves 8 to 12

Red Lentil Hummus

Whether used as a dip, a topping or in a sandwich, this hummus is an inspired riff on a familiar favourite and easily stakes a claim in chickpea territory. This recipe makes a big batch, but the hummus freezes beautifully—perfect for impromptu gatherings.

Roasted garlic Preheat oven to 350°F.

Place garlic in a small ovenproof container or on a piece of aluminum foil. Drizzle oil overtop until fully coated. Roast for 30 minutes, or until garlic is soft and spreadable. Set aside.

Red lentil hummus Place lentils in a strainer and pick out debris and discoloured lentils. Rinse under cold running water, then transfer to a large saucepan. Pour in 6 cups water and bring to a boil. Reduce heat to a gentle simmer and cook for 15 to 20 minutes, until all the water is absorbed. (Add more water, if necessary.)

In a saucepan, combine wine, garlic, roasted garlic and tomatoes and simmer over medium heat for 2 minutes. Add lentils and cook, stirring frequently, for 15 minutes, or until lentils are completely tender.

Stir in oil, coriander, vinegar, salt and chipotle powder. Working in batches, transfer mixture to a blender and purée until smooth. Set aside to cool. Once cooled, stir in the sumac. (If the mixture is too hot, the sumac will turn grey.) Transfer to a serving bowl and serve with pickled vegetables, chips, crudité, bread or crackers.

Sidewalk Citizen Bakery
Aviv Fried and Michal Lavi

His bakeries are devoted to organic, hand-cut sourdough breads and quality deli products. There are now locations in Kensington and another in the East Village's historic Simmons Building, which became a morning hotspot thanks to dishes such as flavoursome shakshuka, spice-laden mezes and fortifying stews. Inspired by the bustling street foods of Israel and the sun-drenched markets of the Levantine, Sidewalk Citizen Bakery takes us on a colourful culinary adventure without having to leave our hometown.

ABOUT THE CHEFS

Born and raised in Israel, Aviv Fried has an impressive set of credentials: not only has he trained internationally with master baker Jeffrey Hamelman of King Arthur Flour, Parisian sourdough master Jean-Luc Poujauran and Chad Robertson of Tartine Bakery, but he also staged at Ottolenghi in London and at Dan Barber's Blue Hill Farm.

Michal Lavi is an award-winning independent filmmaker who has written and directed six short films that have screened in over 40 international and national film festivals. In January 2016, Lavi started Tzavta, a monthly cultural dinner salon that brings together creative thinkers from around the world and has hosted guests such as Man Booker Prize winner George Saunders and physicist Michael Landry.

Sidewalk Citizen Bakery began as a one-man bike operation. Aviv Fried baked and delivered sourdough loaves on his bike, donating the proceeds to charity. After word got out and his reputation for making exceptional artisanal bread had been established, the demand grew, eventually taking him from bike basket to farmers' markets to his first brick-and-mortar.

The bakery's name was inspired by Jane Jacobs's book *The Death and Life of Great American Cities*. "The book identifies the vital role of small business in creating community, fostering human interaction, generating ideas and creativity, and making the city an exciting and a safe place to live," says partner Michal Lavi. "This busy, symbiotic interaction between people and retail was described as an intricate 'sidewalk ballet,' and we always wanted to be a part of that dance."

Roasted beets

3 large golden beets, washed
1 Tbsp extra-virgin olive oil, for coating
Kosher salt, to taste

Red fife

1 Tbsp kosher salt
1 cup red fife wheat berries

Rainbow chard

1 head rainbow chard

Sumac dressing

1 tsp sumac
1 tsp dried oregano
1 tsp dried fenugreek leaves
½ cup freshly squeezed lemon juice
2 tsp honey
1 cup extra-virgin olive oil
Kosher salt, to taste

Assembly

1 English cucumber
½ red onion, thinly sliced
Kosher salt, to taste
Za'atar, for sprinkling

Red Fife Wheat Berries, Golden Beets, Rainbow Chard and Sumac Dressing

Serves 4 to 6

We like the sweetness of golden beets, rather than the common red ones, for this colourful salad. The recipe makes more dressing than required for this dish, so store leftovers in the refrigerator to use on salads.

Roasted beets Preheat oven to 375°F.

Trim beet tops, leaving ¼-inch stem and root intact. Coat beets in oil, season with salt and roast for 45 to 60 minutes, until they can be easily pierced with a knife. Set aside to cool.

Red fife Fill a saucepan with water, add salt and bring to a boil. Add red fife, reduce heat to medium-low and cover. Simmer for 30 to 60 minutes, until the wheat berries are tender and chewy. Add more water, if necessary, to keep the red fife submerged. Drain, then set aside to cool.

Rainbow chard Wash and dry chard using dish towels. Thinly slice chard, reserving the stems for another use, like a stir-fry or vegetable soup.

Sumac dressing In a medium bowl, combine sumac, oregano, fenugreek and lemon juice. Set aside for at least 30 minutes.

Using a small strainer, strain mixture into a small bowl and discard the herbs. Stir in honey, then slowly whisk in oil until mixture is emulsified. Season with salt to taste.

Assembly Using a paring knife, remove beet skins. Cut beets into bite-sized pieces and set aside.

Cut cucumbers in half lengthwise, then cut each half again lengthwise. Run knife along the white line where the seeds meet the flesh and remove the seeds. Cut each length diagonally in a ½-inch thickness. Set aside. Peel and slice onion in half, cutting across the grain to make thin half-rounds.

In a large bowl, combine beets, red fife, chard, cucumber, onion, a couple of pinches of salt and your desired amount of sumac dressing.

Place on a serving platter and sprinkle with za'atar.

Puff pastry

1 tsp freshly squeezed lemon juice

5 cups organic unbleached white flour, plus extra for dusting

1 cup (2 sticks) + 2 Tbsp unsalted butter (divided)

1 tsp kosher salt

Filling

⅓ cup crumbled feta

⅓ cup shredded aged cheddar

1 large egg, beaten

Sesame seeds

Green harissa

2 fresh jalapeño peppers, stemmed and seeded

1 tsp cumin seeds

6 cloves garlic

1 bunch cilantro

⅔ bunch Italian parsley

5 green onions

Juice of ½ lemon

1 tsp white vinegar

⅓ cup extra-virgin olive oil

⅓ cup grapeseed oil

Kosher salt, to taste

Assembly

3 ripe tomatoes

8 fried or hard-boiled eggs

Burekas with Cheddar, Feta, Tomato, Egg and Green Harissa

Serves 8

A Mediterranean breakfast staple, burekas are puff pastry pockets filled with creamy feta and sharp cheddar. Decadent, satisfying and messy, it is more than the sum of its parts. Here, the recipe uses a simplified version of Sidewalk Citizen Bakery's dough, but if you're pressed for time, you can also use a high-quality store-bought puff pastry.

Puff pastry In a stand mixer fitted with the hook attachment, combine lemon juice and 1 cup cold water. Add flour, 2 tablespoons warm butter and salt and mix on low speed for 2 to 3 minutes, until combined into a soft, pliable dough. (Add a little more water if the dough is too dry.) Roll into a ball, wrap in plastic wrap and chill in the refrigerator for 30 minutes.

Take the remaining butter out of the refrigerator and set aside to soften until malleable. Using a rolling pin, roll butter to a ½-inch-thick sheet. Chill in the refrigerator for 15 minutes. Remove from the refrigerator and set aside for 5 to 10 minutes, until soft enough that when your thumb is pressed into it, a shallow impression remains.

On a lightly floured work surface, roll dough into a ¼-inch-thick square. Place the sheeted butter in the centre of the dough and fold the sides over the butter (so the two sides meet at the centre). Roll dough and butter into a square ⅛ inch thick. (It's fine if it ends up rectangular.)

Starting at one end, fold a third to the centre, then fold over the other end to cover. Turn dough 90 degrees and roll again into a ¼-inch-thick square. Cut into eight 2½-inch squares.

Filling In a small bowl, combine cheeses. Place a spoonful in the centre of a dough square, then fold the dough into a triangle. Using your fingers, press down the edges. (You should have a triangular-shaped pocket with a "belly" of cheese.) Brush the pocket with egg and sprinkle with sesame seeds. Place on a baking sheet lined with parchment paper. Repeat with the remaining dough and filling. Burekas can be frozen at this stage (see Note).

Green harissa In a food processor, pulse jalapeños, cumin, garlic, cilantro, parsley and green onions until a rough paste forms. (Add a little water, if necessary.) Add lemon juice, vinegar and both oils and mix until well combined. Season with salt. Set aside. (Harissa can be kept in a sealed container in the refrigerator up to 1 month.)

Assembly Preheat oven to 350°F.

Bake burekas on the prepared baking sheet for 30 minutes, or until golden and puffy.

While the burekas are baking, grate tomatoes. Trim off ends and grate tomatoes into a bowl. (This gives them an interesting texture.) Discard the peel.

Cut the hot burekas open and insert a fried egg or sliced hard-boiled egg into each. Serve immediately with a side of grated tomato and green harissa.

Pictured | p. 173

Starbelly Open Kitchen + Lounge
Derek Mihalik

To keep things fresh and local, almost everything is sourced within a hundred kilometres of the restaurant and the menu changes seasonally. The restaurant's careful attention extends also to the inventive cocktails, such as the Oaxacan Old Fashioned, made with mezcal, charred cedar bitters, rich simple syrup and charred orange.

ABOUT THE CHEF

Originally from Lethbridge, Derek Mihalik grew up on his mom's home-cooked meals made from farmers' market meat and produce. Her cooking style had a huge influence on Mihalik, and he knew from a young age that he wanted to be a chef. Self-taught, he started working in restaurants when he was 17. Working his way through the larger chain restaurants, he learned the business side of running a restaurant. Mihalik has been at the helm of Starbelly for three years, responsible for charting the culinary direction of the menu, training staff and ensuring excellent service. He draws on fresh local ingredients for dishes like the beet salad and the sous vide pork chop. Occasionally he'll use local ingredients to recreate a dish he's discovered while travelling (such as the Çilbir Ghetto Benny, p. 178).

"I still have a close bond with the Hutterite farmers who come to visit us at the restaurant and bring products for us to cook with," says Mihalik. "That's what makes Starbelly special."

Starbelly operates by a simple philosophy: "Your community, our kitchen." Located in Seton, this fun and unique restaurant has a clear focus: to stay true to its local roots by cooking dishes with all that Alberta has to offer. Starbelly's warm, welcoming atmosphere is enhanced by the restaurant's willingness to accommodate food allergies and vegan menu requests. For those on the paleo diet, there's now steak tartare, made with Alberta beef, horseradish aioli, hot sauce, sumac, preserved lemon, rosewater and orange blossom water. If you like your meat cooked, the Starbelly Burger is a hands-down customer favourite, made with eight ounces ground beef and topped with bacon, fancy sauce, fried onions, aged white cheddar, lettuce and tomato.

▶ Çilbir Ghetto Benny | p. 178

Garlic-dill yogurt

2 cups plain full-fat yogurt
¼ cup finely chopped dill
1 Tbsp fine sea salt
1 Tbsp freshly ground black pepper
2 cloves garlic, chopped

Chimichurri

¼ cup extra-virgin olive oil
¼ cup red wine vinegar
¼ cup coarsely chopped cilantro
¼ cup coarsely chopped Italian
  parsley
¼ cup coarsely chopped mint leaves
¼ cup coarsely chopped green onions
¼ tsp red chili flakes
1 large clove garlic, finely chopped

Cajun butter

1 cup (2 sticks) unsalted butter,
  room temperature
1 Tbsp brown sugar
1 Tbsp fine sea salt
1 Tbsp chili powder
1 Tbsp dried basil
1 Tbsp smoked paprika
1½ tsp finely ground black pepper
1½ tsp cayenne pepper
1½ tsp garlic powder
1½ tsp dried oregano
1½ tsp dried thyme

Serves 4

Çilbir Ghetto Benny

Turkish *çilbir* is a delicious dish of poached eggs with yogurt and Aleppo pepper. Derek Mihalik's adventurous twist on tradition teams these classic elements with fresh herbs, sweet and spicy Cajun butter and sourdough toast. The Cajun butter recipe makes a large log, perfect since it can be added to anything that needs a spicy, salty, sweet butter compound, from roast chicken to hot-off-the-grill steak.

Garlic-dill yogurt In a medium bowl, fold together all ingredients to combine. Set aside.

Chimichurri In a blender, purée all ingredients until smooth. Set aside. (This can also be made a few hours in advance and kept in the refrigerator.)

Cajun butter In a stand mixer fitted with the paddle attachment, whip butter on high speed for 3 to 4 minutes, until butter is smooth and doubled in volume. Using a spatula, scrape down the sides of the bowl to push butter into the centre. Add the remaining ingredients and mix on low speed until thoroughly combined. Set aside ¼ cup butter.

Place a long sheet of plastic wrap on a work surface and place the remaining butter on top in a long strip, about 1½ inches in diameter. Roll butter in the plastic wrap into a log, then freeze.

Chipotle salt
1 Tbsp fine sea salt
1 Tbsp chipotle powder
2 tsp brown sugar

Poached eggs
2 Tbsp white vinegar
8 eggs, room temperature

Assembly
Slice of toasted sourdough

Chipotle salt In a small bowl, combine ingredients and set aside.

Poached eggs Fill a saucepan a third full with water and bring to a simmer over medium heat.

Add vinegar to pan. Crack an egg into a small measuring cup or ramekin. Carefully place egg in the centre of the pan. Using a whisk or spoon, stir the water in one direction, creating a whirlpool effect. (This helps the egg white wrap around the egg yolk—it only works when you cook one or two eggs at a time.) Cook for 2 to 3 minutes for a soft-poached egg. Using a slotted spoon, transfer egg to a plate lined with paper towel. Repeat with the remaining eggs.

Assembly Scoop ½ cup garlic-dill yogurt into each of four serving bowls and spread evenly over the bottom. Spoon a tablespoon of chimichurri on one side of the yogurt and a tablespoon of Cajun butter on the other side. Gently set two poached eggs in the centre. Place a slice of sourdough on the side.

Season the eggs with a generous sprinkling of chipotle salt and serve immediately.

Pictured | p. 177

Salted caramel sauce
2 cups granulated sugar

1 cup whipping cream

6 Tbsp unsalted butter, cut into ½-inch cubes

1 Tbsp fine sea salt

2 Tbsp hazelnut liqueur (or your liqueur of choice)

Sticky toffee pudding
2 cups quality pitted dates (preferably Deglet Noor)

2 cups hot freshly brewed coffee

1 Tbsp baking soda

¾ cup (1½ sticks) unsalted butter, room temperature

¼ cup granulated sugar

¼ cup packed brown sugar

1 egg yolk

2 egg whites

1 cup all-purpose flour

1 Tbsp Dutch process cocoa powder

1½ tsp baking powder

1 tsp fine sea salt

Cooking spray

Assembly
Vanilla ice cream or gelato, to serve

Sticky Toffee Pudding with Caramel Sauce

Serves 6

This sticky toffee pudding is the perfect marriage of chocolate, moist cake, vanilla bean gelato and toffee flavour. The Starbelly team wanted to create something that would rival their top-selling doughnut and a new favourite was born!

Salted caramel sauce In a large saucepan, combine sugar and ½ cup water over medium heat. Stir until sugar is dissolved and mixture starts to bubble. Increase heat to high and bring mixture to a boil. Leave untouched and boil for 6 to 8 minutes, until it's a dark amber colour. Immediately remove from heat.

Slowly and carefully whisk in cream until mixture froths up and quadruples in size. Add butter and salt and whisk until everything is incorporated and butter is melted.

Pour the salted caramel sauce into a heatproof bowl or dish and set aside to cool. Stir in hazelnut liqueur.

Sticky toffee pudding Preheat oven to 350°F.

In a large saucepan, combine dates and coffee. Set aside for 15 minutes to allow dates to soften, then purée in a blender until smooth.

Transfer mixture to the saucepan and bring to a light simmer over medium heat. Simmer, stirring occasionally, for 5 minutes, or until a thick paste forms. Remove pan from heat and whisk in baking soda. (The mixture will foam up.) Set aside to cool to room temperature.

Meanwhile, in a stand mixer fitted with the paddle attachment, mix butter with both sugars on low speed for 1 minute. Increase speed to medium and mix for another 2 minutes, or until smooth and creamy.

Add egg yolk and egg whites and mix on low speed until fully incorporated. Using a spatula, scrape sides of the bowl.

In a separate bowl, sift together flour, cocoa powder, baking powder and salt, then whisk to evenly mix. Stir dry ingredients into the butter mixture in three batches. Add date mixture and mix on low speed until combined. Using a spatula, scrape sides of the bowl and mix again.

Spray a 6-cup muffin pan or individual ramekins with cooking spray. Scoop ¾ cup mixture into each cup, leaving ½ inch of space at the top. Bake for 25 minutes, or until a tooth-pick inserted into the centre of the pudding comes out clean.

Assembly Place a pudding on a plate, add ice cream (or gelato) and drizzle with 2 tablespoons salted caramel sauce. Serve immediately.

Teatro Ristorante
Matthew Batey

And no experience at the restaurant would be complete without an order of the tiramisu. Created by Teatro founder Dario Berloni's mother, this dessert hits all the right notes. And best of all, it represents the familial thread that binds the fabric of the Teatro Group.

ABOUT THE CHEF

By the time he was age 14, corporate executive chef Matthew Batey knew he'd be a chef. After completing an apprenticeship at the Fairmont Empress hotel, Batey was promptly recruited to open Catch, recognized in 2002 by *enRoute* magazine as Canada's Best New Restaurant. His passion for regional cuisine led him to The Terrace Restaurant at Mission Hill Family Estate winery, where he developed his repertoire further with the bounty of the Okanagan Valley.

In 2014, Batey returned to Calgary to work on the development of The Nash and Off Cut Bar in Inglewood, becoming involved in the conceptual and operational design of the restaurant.

Today, as corporate executive chef for Teatro Group Restaurants, he oversees the culinary direction of the group's seven distinctive restaurants. He has been fortunate to represent Canada in several international culinary competitions, garnering gold medals and one world championship. "There is no greater honour than wearing the maple leaf and representing your country," he tells us. "I just do it with a knife rather than a stick."

Teatro represents 25 years of restaurant history and quality, rooted in the cuisine of Italy. The Teatro Group has seven stand-alone restaurants, each representing a different concept and cuisine with high-quality food and service that's become synonymous with its name.

Located in the 1911 neoclassical Dominion Bank building downtown, Teatro's beautiful dining room boasts a lush, intimate and slightly hedonistic vibe: 20-foot-high ceilings supported by massive Corinthian columns, a collection of contemporary Canadian art and a chandelier that could be part of any art installation. The seasonal menu highlights local produce, meats and house-made pastas inspired by culinary traditions of Northern Italy, while the award-winning wine list will impress the most discerning of wine experts.

Rapini pesto

1 cup rapini florets
¼ cup extra-virgin olive oil
1 cup basil leaves
¼ cup pine nuts, lightly toasted
1 clove garlic
2 Tbsp grated Parmesan

Gnocchi

1 lb potatoes, such as Agria or Yukon Gold
4 large eggs
Grated zest and juice of 1 lemon
1 Tbsp chopped tarragon
1 Tbsp chopped Italian parsley
1 Tbsp chopped chives
3⅓ cups all-purpose white flour, plus extra for dusting
Olive oil, for greasing
2 Tbsp kosher salt, plus extra for lining a baking sheet

Assembly

½ cup (1 stick) unsalted butter
4 shallots, sliced
2 pears, peeled and diced
1 tsp chopped Italian parsley
1 tsp chopped tarragon
1 tsp chopped thyme
Vanilla salt, for sprinkling (see Note)
Shaved Parmesan, for garnish

Gnocchi with Charred Rapini Pesto, Warmed Pear and Vanilla Salt

Serves 4 to 6

What's not to love about this dish? These silky smooth and textured gnocchi are the perfect vehicle for a bold rapini pesto. The potatoes must be baked (rather than boiled) so that the flesh is dry, and thereby reducing the amount of flour needed for the dough. Teatro bakes potatoes on a bed of salt for added flavour and to prevent colouring. The salt can be reused for roasting beets, carrots or celeriac.

Rapini pesto In a large bowl, toss rapini with oil.

Preheat a grill over high heat. Add rapini, reserving oil, and grill for 5 minutes, turning, or until charred on all sides. Remove from heat.

In a food processor, blend rapini, basil, pine nuts and garlic to a coarse paste. Add cheese, then slowly drizzle in reserved oil until completely incorporated. (Do not allow the blender to heat up, as this will cause pesto to discolour.)

Refrigerate until needed.

Gnocchi Preheat oven to 350°F.

Line a baking sheet with ½ inch of salt, lay whole potatoes on top and bake for 45 minutes, or until the potatoes can be easily pierced with a fork. Set aside until just cool enough to handle.

Peel potatoes. Using a ricer, rice potatoes into a bowl. (Alternatively, mash them if you don't have a ricer.) Transfer potatoes to a lightly floured work surface and create a well in the centre.

In a separate bowl, mix eggs, lemon zest and juice and chopped herbs with a fork to thoroughly combine. Transfer to the potato well and, using your hands, gently mix.

Add half the flour and mix until the dough is slightly tacky but not tacky enough to stick to a floured work surface. Add more flour if necessary. (Do not overwork the dough or add too much flour, or gnocchi will be tough.)

NOTE: Vanilla salt can be purchased at specialty food stores or made by storing a vanilla bean in a jar of Maldon salt for 1 week.

Line a baking sheet with parchment paper. On a floured work surface, roll out the dough into a long strip, ½ inch in diameter. Dipping a knife in flour as needed to prevent sticking, cut dough into ½-inch segments. Place gnocchi on the prepared baking sheet, making sure they aren't touching. If desired, roll gnocchi on a gnocchi paddle or press the back of a fork into the pieces to create small grooves. (These grooves are great for holding sauce but not essential.)

Grease another baking sheet. Bring a large saucepan of water to an aggressive boil and add salt. Reduce heat slightly and immediately add gnocchi, working in batches to avoid over-crowding. Cook for 5 minutes, or until gnocchi float to the surface. Using a slotted spoon, gently transfer to the prepared baking sheet. Repeat with the remaining gnocchi.

Assembly Melt butter in a large saucepan over medium-high heat. Add gnocchi and cook until lightly browned. Add shallots and cook for 2 minutes, or until translucent. Add pears and sauté for 1 minute, or until just heated through.

Remove from heat and divide gnocchi mixture among warm bowls. Top with a spoonful of rapini pesto, a pinch each of parsley, tarragon and thyme, a sprinkle of vanilla salt and shaved Parmesan to taste. Serve immediately.

Mascarpone gelato

⅓ cup whole milk

2 egg yolks

1 vanilla bean, split and scraped

⅓ cup granulated sugar

3 Tbsp mascarpone

Almond cake

1¾ cups (3½ sticks) unsalted butter, room temperature, plus extra for greasing

¾ cup granulated sugar

4 large eggs

2 cups almond flour

1⅓ cups all-purpose flour

1 Tbsp baking powder

Assembly

6½ Tbsp Marsala

Cocoa powder, for dusting

Vanilla ice cream, to serve

6 Tbsp espresso, room temperature

½ cup raspberry coulis (optional)

¼ cup shaved dark chocolate

Serves 4 to 6

Teatro Tiramisu

Teatro owner Dario Berloni's late mother, Mirella, generously shared her long-standing family tiramisu recipe with all seven Teatro properties, but here, her traditional dessert is reimagined by pastry chef Daniel Ramon. We recommend using a candy thermometer and ice-cream maker for this recipe.

Mascarpone gelato Gently heat milk in a saucepan over medium heat. Be careful to not scorch it or you'll need to start over.

In a medium bowl, combine egg yolks, vanilla seeds and sugar. Slowly whisk in the scalded milk to bring the egg mixture up to the same temperature as the milk. Pour mixture into the saucepan and cook over medium heat to a temperature of 80°F, stirring continuously to prevent eggs from overcooking. Remove from heat and whisk in mascarpone.

Fill a bowl with ice water and place another bowl on top. Strain mixture through a fine-mesh sieve into the top bowl and set aside for 1 hour, or until thoroughly chilled.

Using an ice-cream maker or a handheld mixer, churn the chilled base into ice cream. Keep in the freezer until ready to use.

Almond cake Preheat oven to 350°F. Line a jellyroll pan or a baking sheet with parchment paper and lightly grease with butter.

In a stand mixer fitted with the paddle attachment, cream butter and sugar. Add eggs, one at a time, mixing until fully incorporated.

In another bowl, sift together both flours and baking powder. Add to the wet mixture and gently mix until fully incorporated.

Pour batter into the prepared pan and bake for 25 minutes, or until the top is golden brown and springy (or until a toothpick inserted into the centre of the cake comes out clean). Set aside until needed.

If the cake isn't used right away, wrap it tightly in plastic wrap to maintain freshness.

Assembly Lightly brush Marsala over the surface of the cake, then dust with cocoa powder. Cut cake into 3-inch circles. Place a scoop of ice cream on each piece of cake, then pour espresso overtop.

Dot with raspberry coulis, if using. Quickly scatter chocolate over ice cream and serve immediately.

Ten Foot Henry
Steve Smee

to exceptional service, a creative menu and an eclectic wine list, Ten Foot Henry stands tall.

"Ten Foot Henry is a little more fast-paced than we might have imagined, challenging us to speed up our cooking techniques and service style, all the while maintaining an impeccable experience for our guests," Smee says. "All things considered, today's Ten Foot Henry definitely lines up with our vision for this project."

ABOUT THE CHEF

Transforming and revolutionizing Calgary's culinary offerings with an imaginative emphasis on vegetables requires a degree of conviction and swagger, and Steve Smee and Aja Lapointe have plenty of both. Lapointe, formerly general manager of UNA Pizza + Wine (p. 196), and Smee, formerly executive chef at UNA, Ox Bar de Tapas (formerly Ox & Angela) and Mercato (p. 132), wanted to strike out on their own and open a restaurant that would reflect their own vision, style and personalities. Smee would design the plant-driven menu and Lapointe would craft the ever-changing wine and cocktail list.

"We are absolutely humbled by the accolades for the restaurant. The support by our community has been nothing short of remarkable," Lapointe reveals. "We truly count our blessings!"

Some chefs will cross oceans and trek thousands of miles in search of culinary inspiration and innovations, whereas others are quite happy to find it at home. The husband-and-wife team behind Ten Foot Henry, Steve Smee and Aja Lapointe, draw many of their ideas from their home cooking. With imaginative dishes such as an updated Caesar salad with chicory, kale, cashews and pecorino, their healthy, vegetable-forward menu bridges the gap between what you should be eating and what you really want to eat.

The duo founded Ten Foot Henry in 2016. They opened the restaurant with a team of seasoned restaurant professionals, many of whom they had worked with in the past. Thanks

Chargrilled carrots

2 lbs tri-coloured carrots, rinsed and trimmed

3 Tbsp extra-virgin olive oil

2 tsp kosher salt

Salsa verde

½ cup Castelvetrano or any mild green olives, pitted

¼ cup capers

1 clove garlic

½ bunch Italian parsley, leaves only

½ bunch mint, leaves only

½ cup olive or canola oil

Grated zest and juice of 1 lemon

Kosher salt, to taste

Assembly

2 ripe avocados, pitted and sliced into wedges

½ cup roasted unsalted hazelnuts, roughly chopped, for garnish

Flaky sea salt

Chargrilled Carrots with Salsa Verde, Avocado and Hazelnuts

Serves 4

Carrots are a permanent fixture on the Ten Foot Henry menu, but the garnishes change with the season. Early summer carrots have a sharp, raw taste that works well with salsa verde, avocado and hazelnuts. The salsa verde can also be made with a variety of soft herbs such as cilantro or tarragon. We recommend doubling up on the recipe and having a jar of this deliciousness on hand to serve with other dishes.

Chargrilled carrots Preheat a grill over medium-low heat.

If carrots are very thick, halve them lengthwise (or leave whole if they are young). In a bowl, toss carrots with oil and salt. Grill carrots on one side for 10 to 15 minutes, then flip and cook for another 10 minutes, or until tender. (Alternatively, place dressed carrots on a baking sheet and roast at 400°F for 20 minutes, or until fork tender but not mushy.)

Salsa verde In a food processor, combine olives, capers and garlic and process until mixed through but still coarse.

Set aside some parsley and mint leaves for garnish. Finely chop the remaining leaves. In a mixing bowl, combine herbs and olive mixture. Stir in oil and lemon zest and juice. Season with salt to taste (since olives and capers are quite briny, salt may not be needed). Store in an airtight container in the refrigerator for up to 2 days.

Assembly Remove the avocado flesh from the skin and place in a mixing bowl with the carrots.

In the mixing bowl, gently toss carrots and avocado with salsa verde. Transfer salad to a serving dish. Sprinkle hazelnuts and parsley and mint leaves overtop. Finish with a pinch of sea salt and serve.

Roasted beets

2 lbs small red or multi-coloured beets, unpeeled and trimmed

Whipped feta

1½ cups Macedonian feta, drained
2 Tbsp freshly squeezed lemon juice
2 Tbsp grated lemon zest

Pistachio dukkah

1 cup pistachios, roasted
1 Tbsp roasted sesame seeds
1 Tbsp ground cumin
1 Tbsp sumac
1 Tbsp dried thyme
1 Tbsp dried oregano
½ tsp kosher salt, plus extra to taste
½ tsp freshly ground black pepper

Assembly

2 Tbsp sherry vinegar
2 Tbsp olive oil
Pinch of sea salt
1 bunch dill, chopped

Roasted Beets with Feta, Lemon, Dill and Pistachio Dukkah

Serves 4

Beets were an inherent part of Steve Smee's childhood and continue to be a staple at family occasions. One notable dish was a rich borscht with warming spices, fresh dill and a subtle sharpness from vinegar; each person would add sour cream to their taste. This cold salad borrows the spirit of that borscht, adding a zip of lemon and aromatic *dukkah*, an Egyptian condiment of herbs, spices and nuts.

Roasted beets Preheat oven to 350°F. Line a baking sheet with parchment paper.

Place beets on the prepared baking sheet and roast for 1 hour, or until fully cooked and a tip of a paring knife can pierce the beets with ease. Set aside to cool completely, then trim the tops where the greens were attached. Cut beets into ½-inch-thick slices. Set aside.

Whipped feta In a food processor, pulse feta until very smooth. Transfer to a bowl and stir in lemon juice and zest. Store in an airtight container in the refrigerator for up to 3 days.

Pistachio dukkah In a food processor, coarsely chop pistachios. Transfer to a mixing bowl.

In a spice grinder, blend the remaining ingredients to a fine powder. (It's okay to have a few chunks of sesame seeds, which will add texture to the dish.) Add spice mix to pistachios and stir to combine. Adjust salt to taste. Store in an airtight container at room temperature for up to 1 week.

Assembly In a large mixing bowl, gently toss beets with vinegar, oil and salt.

Spread a generous amount of whipped feta onto the bottom of a serving dish. Arrange beets on top, and sprinkle dukkah and chopped dill overtop.

Two Penny /
The Tea House
Cody Willis

delightful wine list featuring bottles to complement the often spicy food.

"Two Penny was born out of a love for Chinese food. Being a seventh-generation Canadian, I don't have any particular cuisine that I identify with as my own," explains Willis, who grew up eating Chinese food as much as he did burgers. "That's why Canada is so special. It's got an amazing multiculturalism and, with that, a variety of cuisines. The food at Two Penny, in its simplest form, reflects the food that we grew up eating and want to eat."

ABOUT THE CHEF

Two Penny is Cody Willis's third successful foray into Calgary's chef-driven food scene. With general manager Andrea Robinson, Willis has created an evocative destination that might be described as a Silk Road watering hole.

Two Penny draws influence from the metropolitan city of Hong Kong, applying a mixture of traditional and modern techniques, flavours and ingredients to familiar Chinese dishes with excellent results.

If you don't want to sit in the upstairs dining room, you can descend the staircase to The Tea House, a dim-lit cocktail den bathed in the red glow of Chinese lanterns tailor-made for intimate gatherings.

Unlike the Chinese restaurants that we grew up with, Two Penny has killer cocktails, and a

Born and raised in Calgary, Cody Willis has been instrumental in putting the fun into dining out. The visionary behind Two Penny—as well as Native Tongues Taqueria (p. 142) and Calcutta Cricket Club (p. 44)—Willis learned classic mixology in London, has travelled across Europe, Asia and Mexico and is a certified sommelier. After attending Stratford Chefs School, he returned to Calgary to work as a cook while organizing pop-up dinners around town with his brother, Jesse. The first experience was a 13-course New Nordic–Canadiana menu, but Willis felt the city needed something more fun and light-hearted—and their second taco-inspired pop-up was just that. "It was exciting to cook, and people loved it," Willis tells us and then adds, "Dining out is entertainment and should be fun."

2 Tbsp canola oil

¼ cup finely chopped garlic

8 oz ground lamb

½ cup Shaoxing cooking wine

½ cup Sichuan oil
(preferably Lao Gan Ma)

½ cup doubanjiang
(preferably Lao Gan Ma)

¼ cup fermented black beans

2 cups chicken stock

1 (15-oz) package medium-firm
tofu, cut into 1-inch cubes

1 tsp cornstarch

½ tsp ground Sichuan pepper,
for garnish

Small handful of chopped
green onions, for garnish

Steamed rice, to serve

*Serves
4 to 6*

Lamb Mapo Tofu

Mapo tofu—a dish hailing the Sichuan province of China—is traditionally prepared with pork or beef and spiced up with a fermented chili pepper and bean sauce known as *doubanjiang*. Here, it's made with Alberta lamb, the strong flavours complementing the spices. The Chinese ingredients are available at Asian supermarkets such as T&T and Lambda Oriental Foods.

Heat oil in a saucepan over medium heat. Add garlic and sauté for 1 minute, or until soft and fragrant. Increase heat to high, add lamb and stir for 2 to 3 minutes, breaking up the larger pieces. Pour in wine and cook for 5 minutes, or until pan is nearly dry. Add oil, doubanjiang, black beans and chicken stock and simmer for 5 minutes, then set aside.

Bring 4 cups salted water to a boil in a medium saucepan. Using a slotted spoon, carefully add tofu, reduce heat to medium-low and simmer for 1 minute, or until tofu is heated through. Using the slotted spoon, carefully transfer tofu to the lamb mapo sauce. Gently cook over medium heat for 2 minutes, or until warmed through.

If the sauce is too runny, combine cornstarch and 3 tablespoons cold water in a small bowl. Pour mixture into pan, a little at a time, and cook for another minute, or until sauce reaches your desired consistency.

Spoon the finished lamb mapo tofu into a large serving bowl. Garnish with ground Sichuan pepper and green onions. Serve with steamed rice.

4 cups chicken stock

2 tsp kosher salt

1 (3- to 5-lb) whole chicken

½ cup Sichuan oil (preferably
   Lao Gan Ma)

¼ cup finely chopped green onions,
   for garnish

2 Tbsp roasted peanuts, for garnish

1 Tbsp sesame seeds, for garnish

1 Tbsp Maldon salt, for garnish

"Mouthwatering" Sichuan Chicken

Serves 2 to 4, as an appetizer

Two Penny gives cold chicken the respect that it deserves. This dish is so good you'll be tempted to skip the niceties and eat it with your fingers, picking it straight off the plate while standing in front of the open refrigerator. Served with Two Penny's signature Sichuan chili oil, this fiery, numbing dish will kick start the appetite.

Bring stock to a boil in a medium saucepan. Add salt and chicken, reduce heat to medium and simmer for 10 minutes, or until chicken is cooked through. Using tongs, transfer it to a bowl and cool in the refrigerator. (The stock can be reserved for another use, such as soups and stews, or reuse it for more cold chicken.)

Separate the legs and split the breasts. Slice chilled chicken into bite-sized pieces. Place chicken in a shallow bowl and cover it generously with oil. Garnish with green onions, peanuts and sesame seeds. Finish with Maldon salt.

UNA Pizza + Wine

Kayle Burns

Nearly a decade after its opening, UNA remains as popular as ever as crowds continue to devour its delicious thin-crust pizzas. Table times are updated by cell phone and social media, giving you the opportunity to tuck into Frenchie Wine Bar—hidden behind UNA Takeaway next door—for a glass of wine and maybe staying for a cheese fondue. UNA's open kitchen, comfortable ambience and excellent food continue to enrich Calgary's vibrant restaurant scene.

ABOUT THE CHEF

Executive chef Kayle Burns oversees the menus for both Bread and Circus Trattoria (p. 30) and UNA Pizza + Wine. Originally from Quebec, Burns discovered his passion and talent for cooking in Switzerland and has since trained in New York, Tokyo, Melbourne and Sydney. Today, he calls Calgary home. His cooking is a celebration of local, simple food and our community, whether he's preparing a batch of homemade apple cider vinegar or working with local urban farmers to cultivate quality produce.

When UNA Pizza + Wine opened in 2010, it was one of a handful of Calgary restaurants to serve informal food while offering an extensive wine list along with great service. Calgarians welcomed it with open arms from the moment the doors were opened.

We love to park ourselves at the bar and while away the time, marvelling at the frenzy behind the counter: cocktails stirred, wines poured, kale chopped and a seemingly never-ending supply of pizza dough rolled. In fact, thousands of pizzas have passed through those ovens. There's a lot of action: the room is buzzy with conversations and it feels slightly chaotic, but in a good way that keeps us coming back.

3 Tbsp extra-virgin olive oil

16 to 20 fresh prawns, peeled and deveined

3 cherry tomatoes, sliced

1 Tbsp garlic purée

2 tsp kosher salt

2 tsp red chili flakes

2 Tbsp freshly squeezed lemon juice

2 Tbsp sambuca

2 tsp thinly sliced basil, for garnish

Focaccia, to serve

Serves 4

Sambuca Prawns

It's an honour to share history—like when watching kids discover Pink Floyd or Iggy Pop. Here, sambuca prawns, a staple of seventies' dinner parties, are rediscovered and resurrected with UNA flair.

Heat oil in a frying pan over medium heat. Add prawns and sauté for 10 minutes, or until nicely browned. Transfer to a plate and set aside.

In the same pan, add tomatoes, garlic purée, salt and chili flakes and sauté for 3 to 5 minutes, until lightly cooked. (Don't let the garlic burn, as it will become bitter and unpleasant tasting.) Carefully add lemon juice and sambuca (the alcohol will cause the mixture to flambé). Cook for 3 minutes, or until liquid is thick and sticky. Add prawns and heat through.

Assembly Arrange prawns on a serving platter. Garnish with basil and serve hot with fresh focaccia, perfect for soaking up the delicious sauce.

UNA Pizza dough

½ tsp instant yeast

1 cup lukewarm (105°F to 110°F) water

1¾ cups "00" flour, plus extra for dusting

2 Tbsp olive oil, plus extra for greasing

1 tsp honey (preferably Chinook)

1 tsp kosher salt

Cornmeal or semolina, for sprinkling

4-maggi pizza

½ cup grated Friulano or Asiago

½ cup grated provolone

1 ball fior di latte

1 tsp freshly ground black pepper

2 Tbsp honey (preferably Chinook)

1 Tbsp truffle oil

2 Tbsp shaved pecorino

Serves 4

4-Maggi Pizza

We've all queued up for UNA's excellent pizza, and now we can make it ourselves too. If you don't have a pizza stone, take the opportunity to buy one while your dough is chilling in the refrigerator. They can be found at Italian specialty stores and many other specialty food stores. The "00" flour can also be found at specialty food stores, but in a pinch, you can replace it with bread or all-purpose flour. Prepare the dough 24 hours in advance, to give it ample time to develop its flavour.

UNA Pizza dough In a small bowl, combine yeast and warm water. Set aside to foam.

In a stand mixer fitted with the hook attachment, combine flour, oil, honey and salt and mix on low speed for 10 minutes, or until dough is soft and pliable.

Lightly oil a bowl and transfer the dough to it. Flip dough to coat entirely. Cover and refrigerate for 24 hours.

Remove dough from refrigerator and set aside for 30 minutes to bring up to room temperature. Punch down dough and cut in half. Roll each half into a ball, cover with a dish towel and set aside until doubled in size.

Using a rolling pin, roll each dough ball into a circular shape. If it keeps springing back and fights the rolling action, cover again and let rest for 5 minutes. Line a baking sheet with parchment paper and sprinkle with cornmeal (or semolina). Place dough rounds on the prepared baking sheet in preparation for the toppings.

4-maggi pizza Place a pizza stone in the oven and preheat oven to 500°F.

Sprinkle Friulano (or Asiago) and provolone over each dough. Tear fior di latte into 8 pieces and place on top of both. Slide the pizzas onto the hot stone in the oven and bake for 8 minutes, or until dough is cooked and slightly puffy and cheese has caramelized.

Remove pizzas from the oven and cut into 8 slices each. Season with pepper, drizzle honey and truffle oil on top of each and finish with pecorino.

The Wednesday Room
Derek Wilkins

So pull on your black leather pants and winklepickers and head over—it's open for lunch, dinner and late-night cocktailing. Start with a Red Rum cocktail, and if things are going well on the date front, make your next cocktail an Afternoon Delight. But if you arrive late in the evening and order a Smoke after Sex, you're just bragging.

ABOUT THE CHEF

Chef Derek Wilkins was born and raised in Calgary. Having chosen between a career in a kitchen and one in oil and gas, Wilkins graduated in 2012 from SAIT's (Southern Alberta Institute of Technology's) culinary program. His mentor, Chef Hayato Okamitsu, encouraged him to intern at Calgary's Rouge Restaurant. After three years there, Wilkins moved to WORKSHOP Kitchen + Culture (p. 212) where he was chef de cuisine. So what brought him to The Wednesday Room? Of the opportunity to be a partner in a cool new restaurant and put years of experience to good use and create exciting menus, Wilkins says, "It was a chance to do something of my own, to stay in town and work and help raise my two beautiful children. I love what I'm doing in the city I grew up in."

If The Wednesday Room feels to you like a set from Stanley Kubrick's *The Shining*, you wouldn't be imagining it. The boldly patterned carpets and beams, plush couches, heavy wooden coffee tables and huge stone fireplace do indeed channel the lobby of the Overlook Hotel. Downstairs, you'll find a cheeky sixties-lounge vibe, complete with vinyl records, comfortable booths and rich wood panelling. The geometric carpet (exactly like the one young Danny rode along on his trike) is illuminated by floor-mounted globe lights. Vintage typewriters and the words "All work and no play..." projected onto the bar mirror complete the look. This is an authentic lounge experience unlike any other in Calgary.

Cured mushrooms

1 cup sliced cremini mushrooms

Kosher salt, to taste

Pljukanci noodles

2 cups bread flour, plus extra
for dusting

1 tsp kosher salt

Truffle cream sauce

2 Tbsp olive oil

2 large cloves garlic, finely chopped

1 Tbsp finely chopped shallot

4 slices shaved prosciutto, torn into
bite-sized pieces

½ cup dry white wine

2 cups whipping cream

½ cup Cured Mushrooms (see here)

1 Tbsp truffle paste

1 tsp truffle oil

¼ cup grated Parmesan

Assembly

1 tsp extra-virgin olive oil

4 slices prosciutto

Kosher salt and freshly ground
pepper, to taste

Grated Parmesan, to sprinkle

Serves 4

Pasta Pljukanci

Pljukanci, which means "little worms" in Croatian, is a type of pasta from Istria on Croatia's northern coastline. The dough can easily be made with a stand mixer, and the pasta is rolled between the palms of your hands. The cured mushrooms need to be made a day in advance, so plan ahead.

Cured mushrooms Make this the day before you need your sauce. Preheat oven to 200°F.

Place mushrooms on a baking sheet, season with salt and bake for 2 hours. Cool and set aside.

Pljukanci noodles In a stand mixer fitted with the hook attachment, combine flour and salt at medium speed. With the motor still running, gradually add 1 cup hot water until a ball of dough forms. Knead for 2 minutes. Turn off mixer and transfer dough to a clean bowl. Cover with a dish towel and set aside to rest for 10 minutes.

Pinch off a thumb-sized piece of dough and roll it between your palms to form a little "worm," about 2 inches in length. Place on a floured baking sheet. Repeat with the remaining dough. Cover with a dish towel to prevent pasta from drying out.

Truffle cream sauce Heat oil in a frying pan over medium heat. Add garlic, shallot and prosciutto and cook for 4 minutes. (Do not brown.)

Pour in wine and cook for 2 minutes, or until evaporated. Add cream, mushrooms, truffle paste, truffle oil and Parmesan, stirring to combine. Reduce heat to medium-low and cook for 5 minutes, or until slightly reduced.

Assembly Heat oil in a frying pan over medium-high heat. Add prosciutto and fry for 10 to 12 minutes, until crispy. Transfer to a cutting board and, using a sharp knife, cut into thin strips.

Bring a saucepan of salted water to a boil. Add noodles and cook for 5 to 7 minutes, until they float to the surface. Drain noodles and add them to the pan of sauce. Toss to coat noodles, then season with salt and pepper.

Transfer the pasta to a large serving platter. Garnish with crispy prosciutto, sprinkle with Parmesan and serve family-style.

▶ Pork Belly Bao | p. 204

Green onion–apple kimchi

4 green onions, cut into thin strips
1 Granny Smith apple, cut into thin strips
¼ Napa cabbage, cut into thin strips
2 ramps or green onions, cut into thin strips
2 Tbsp gochujang
2 Tbsp rice vinegar
2 Tbsp mirin
2 Tbsp gochugaru
1 Tbsp kosher salt

Braised pork belly

½ onion, coarsely chopped
1 carrot, coarsely chopped
½ fennel bulb, coarsely chopped
1 cup pork stock or water
½ cup soy sauce
¼ cup packed brown sugar
2 star anise
3 lbs pork belly, skin on

Bao buns

1 Tbsp dry active yeast
¼ cup granulated sugar
1¼ cups lukewarm (105°F to 110°F) water
4 cups all-purpose flour, plus extra if needed
2 tsp kosher salt

Serves 6 to 8

Pork Belly Bao

Sweet, savoury pork in a pillow-y bun, pork belly bao encapsulates everything that's right with the world, and this recipe is a guaranteed crowd-pleaser. *Gochugaru*, or Korean chili flakes, are vibrantly red, coarse in texture and subtly sweet. They can be found at Asian supermarkets. We recommend preparing this dish a day in advance, since you'll need to marinate the pork belly and green onion–apple kimchi (which only get better with time).

Green onion–apple kimchi In a large bowl, combine green onions, apple, cabbage and ramps (or more green onions). Add the remaining ingredients and mix well. Refrigerate until needed, preferably overnight.

Braised pork belly Preheat oven to 325°F.

Place onion, carrot and fennel in a deep roasting pan. Add stock (or water), soy sauce, brown sugar and star anise and stir. Place pork belly in pan, skin side up. The liquid should reach two-thirds of the way up the side of the pork belly (if necessary, add more stock or water).

Wrap entire roasting pan tightly with aluminum foil and braise pork belly in the oven for 4 hours. Remove pan from the oven, let cool, then chill in the refrigerator overnight. Portion pork into 2-inch pieces, each ½ inch thick. Set aside. Skim fat off braising liquid and reserve, discarding the solids.

Bao buns In a large bowl, combine yeast, sugar and lukewarm water. Set aside for 5 minutes to foam.

Add 4 cups flour and salt to the bowl and mix well to combine. Form the dough into a ball and knead for 5 minutes, or until soft and silky. (Add more flour, if needed.) Transfer dough to a clean, dry bowl and cover with a damp dish towel until dough has doubled in size.

Meanwhile, cut twenty 2-inch squares of parchment paper. Line a baking sheet with one sheet of parchment paper.

Black sesame aioli

½ cup mayonnaise

2 tsp kosher salt, plus extra to taste

2 tsp freshly squeezed lime juice,
   plus extra if needed

½ tsp sesame oil

½ tsp black sesame paste

½ tsp squid ink

Assembly

1 Tbsp canola oil

Cilantro, for garnish

Roasted peanuts, for garnish

Place dough on a floured work surface and roll to a ½-inch thickness. Using a 2-inch round cookie cutter, cut out disks. Fold over a disk to form a half-moon shape, with a piece of the parchment paper between the two folded sides to prevent them from sticking together. Place folded dough on the prepared baking sheet. Repeat with the remaining dough disks, then loosely cover them with plastic wrap and set aside for 30 minutes to rise.

Line a bamboo steamer with parchment paper. Gently place the buns on the parchment and steam over high heat for 10 minutes. Remove buns from the steamer and set aside to cool. (The buns can be kept in an airtight container in the fridge for up to 5 days. Reheat by steaming for 5 minutes, or pop in a microwave.)

Black sesame aioli In a large bowl, whisk together all ingredients. Taste and adjust seasoning.

Assembly Heat oil in a frying pan over medium-high heat. Add pork belly and pan-fry for 4 minutes on each side.

Spread 1 teaspoon aioli on one side of the bun. Top the other side with 1 tablespoon kimchi. Place a piece of crispy pork belly centred overtop.

Continue until all the buns are filled. Serve family-style on a large platter, garnished with cilantro and roasted peanuts.

Pictured | p. 203

WinSport
Liana Robberecht and Jason McKay

Liana Robberecht is a strong visionary who combines food and art, which keeps her at the forefront of innovation. She was the first female executive chef at Calgary's Petroleum Club, holding that position for over 10 years. She was also instrumental in bringing the first Canadian conference of Women Chefs & Restaurateurs to Calgary, for which she is vice-president. She has participated in Women of the Wild West, the James Beard Foundation dinner, and the eighth Cook It Raw Alberta, among other events. In 2011, Robberecht was named Chef of the Year by the Alberta Foodservice Expo and Canadian Restaurant and Foodservice News, and she is a regular contributor to CBC Radio. "Being a chef is a position of change rather than of authority," Robberecht explains. She certainly does lead by example.

Jason McKay, WinSport's director of Food and Beverage/Sales, has the best job in the world: merging food and sport culture. "There's never a dull moment, and every day is different," he says. And McKay's infectious spirit and enthusiasm for what he does—whether it's hiking a cake to the top of the half-pipe for a celebration or organizing a chairlift dinner or black-tie fundraiser—makes the job fun.

WinSport is a not-for-profit organization. "That's the most rewarding of all—they inspire us, and we help them achieve their dreams of standing on the podium for Canada."

Located at Calgary Olympic Park, one of Calgary's most recognized landmarks, WinSport is an all-in-one ski resort, multi-purpose training and competition facility. With two kitchens and two lounges, WinSport has the skill, space, people and flexibility to host events for up to three thousand people, and it can help with entertainment, decor and audiovisuals.

If you are there for a day of skiing, snowboarding, hiking or biking, stop in for a hot lunch at the Garden Café; the Molson Canadian Hockey House opens at 4 p.m. WinSport prides itself on its fresh, ethically sourced food, and accommodation of allergies and menu requests, while maintaining excellent service onsite and at the hundreds of catered events it does every year. In fact, it was named Best Caterer at the 2016–17 Calgary Event Awards.

Caramelized onion jam

2 Tbsp canola oil (preferably Highwood Crossing)

3 sweet onions, thinly sliced

2 Tbsp granulated sugar

Pinch of ground star anise

1 tsp kosher salt, plus extra to taste

¾ cup port or heavy red wine

2 bay leaves

1 sprig rosemary

1 sprig thyme

1 Tbsp apple cider vinegar

Sauce

½ cup sour cream

Grated zest of 1 lemon

Pinch of ground coriander

Pumpkin–wild rice cakes

⅓ cup wild rice (yields 1 cup cooked)

1 Tbsp kosher salt, plus extra to taste

1 green onion, finely chopped

¼ cup pumpkin purée

¼ tsp grated ginger

¼ tsp ground cumin

Pinch of ground allspice

½ cup all-purpose flour

1 large egg

¼ cup canola oil, for frying

Assembly

1 bunch Italian parsley, stems removed and finely chopped, for garnish

Serves 4 to 6 (makes 12 to 16 mini cakes)

Pumpkin–Wild Rice Cakes with Caramelized Sweet Onion Jam

This recipe is deceptively easy to prepare and makes for the perfect light lunch. It does take some time to cook, so please just trust in your stove to do its job (and perhaps sip a glass of wine while you wait). Caramelizing the onions will extract their deep, rich umami flavour that pairs so well with the rice cakes.

Caramelized onion jam Heat oil in a large frying pan over medium-high heat. Add onions, sugar, star anise and salt and sauté for 15 to 20 minutes, until onions are golden brown. Add port (or red wine), bay leaves, rosemary and thyme and cook for another 20 minutes, or until thickened and liquid has evaporated. Add vinegar and adjust the seasoning. Set aside.

Sauce In a bowl, stir together all ingredients to combine. Transfer to a large squeeze bottle. Set aside.

Pumpkin–wild rice cakes Bring a large saucepan of water to a boil. Add wild rice and salt, reduce heat to medium-low and simmer for 45 minutes to 1 hour, until grains begin to open and rice is tender but chewy. Drain, then set aside to cool.

In a large mixing bowl, combine cooled wild rice, green onion, pumpkin purée, ginger, cumin and allspice. Add flour and egg, mixing gently so the rice grains remain intact.

Heat a drizzle of oil in a large non-stick frying pan over medium-high heat. In batches to avoid overcrowding in the pan, shape wild rice mixture into 2-tablespoon mounds and add to pan. Using a spatula, lightly press down on each mound. Cook for 4 to 5 minutes. Flip over and cook for another 4 to 5 minutes, until crispy and golden brown.

Transfer cakes to a plate, season with salt and set aside. Repeat with the remaining batches.

Assembly Place pumpkin–wild rice cakes on a serving platter. Top each with a dime-sized dot of sauce and a teaspoon of caramelized onions. Sprinkle parsley overtop and serve family-style.

▶ Roasted Red Pepper and Squash Curd, Toasted
Seeds and Seasonal Greens | p. 210

Roasted pepper

Olive oil, for greasing
1 red bell pepper

Squash curd

1 small butternut squash, peeled, seeded and diced
½ Roasted Pepper (see here)
1 Tbsp grated ginger, plus extra to taste
Juice of 1 lemon, plus extra to taste
½ cup honey (preferably Chinook Honey)
½ cup canola oil (preferably Highwood Crossing)
4 large eggs
6 large egg yolks
1 tsp kosher salt, plus extra to taste

Seed mixture

1 Tbsp black sesame seeds
1 Tbsp poppy seeds
1 Tbsp sunflower seeds
1 Tbsp pumpkin seeds
1 Tbsp coriander seeds
1 Tbsp anise seeds
1 Tbsp hemp hearts
¼ cup granulated sugar
Pinch of sea salt

Roasted Red Pepper and Squash Curd, Toasted Seeds and Seasonal Greens

Serves 4

Robust, flavourful and easy to assemble, together this roasted squash and beautiful green salad are an ode to the high quality of our local ingredients.

Roasted pepper Preheat oven to 400°F. Lightly grease a baking sheet.

Place pepper on the prepared baking sheet and roast for 20 minutes. Turn pepper and roast again for another 20 minutes, or until skin is soft and charred and pepper has slightly collapsed. Remove from heat, cover with plastic wrap and set aside for 10 minutes. Peel off skin, then remove stem and seeds. Set aside.

Squash curd Place squash in a medium saucepan and add just enough water to cover. Simmer, uncovered, over medium heat for 25 minutes, or until squash is tender. Drain.

In a blender, blend squash with roasted pepper until smooth. Add ginger, lemon juice, honey and oil and purée. Scrape mixture into a stainless-steel bowl and refrigerate for 30 minutes, or until cooled. Blend in eggs and egg yolks.

Heat a saucepan filled halfway with water over medium heat. Place the stainless-steel bowl on top of the saucepan and whisk squash mixture for 20 minutes, or until thickened. (Don't worry if the curd looks a little like scrambled eggs.)

Transfer to a blender and purée until smooth. Add salt, then adjust seasoning to taste with salt, lemon and ginger. Pour curd into a large squeeze bottle, setting aside extra curd in a small bowl for plating.

Seasonal greens

2 bunches baby arugula
   (pat dry if damp)

4 radishes, thinly sliced

¼ sweet onion, thinly sliced

¼ cup olive or canola oil (preferably
   Highwood Crossing)

Grated zest of 1 lemon

Juice of ½ lemon

2 Tbsp apple cider vinegar

Kosher salt and freshly ground
   black pepper, to taste

Roasted acorn squash

1 acorn squash

Kosher salt and freshly ground
   black pepper, to taste

Seed mixture Combine seeds and hemp hearts in a frying pan over medium heat and lightly toast for 2 to 3 minutes, swirling the pan so they toast evenly and don't burn. Increase heat to high and sprinkle sugar over seeds. Cook for 1 to 2 minutes, stirring continuously, until sugar melts.

Spread seeds in a single layer on a baking sheet lined with parchment paper and season with salt. Set aside to cool completely. Seed mixture can be stored in an airtight container up to 4 weeks.

Seasonal greens In a mixing bowl, toss together all ingredients. Adjust seasoning to taste.

Roasted acorn squash Preheat oven to 325°F.

Wash squash. Place on a baking sheet and roast for 25 minutes. Set aside to cool.

Cut the squash in half and remove seeds. Following the natural ridges of the squash, slice it into as many pieces as there are ridges. (Leave the skin on; it's very tasty.) Season the squash with salt and pepper and set aside for plating.

Assembly Using the curd in the squeeze bottle, draw on each plate several large concentric circles that are larger than the acorn squash pieces. Place squash slightly off-centre between the innermost and outermost curd circles.

Place greens in the centre of each plate. Garnish with toasted seeds.

Pictured | p. 209

WORKSHOP
Kitchen + Culture
Kenny Kaechele

offers catering. To no surprise, WORKSHOP has been ranked one of the 100 Best Restaurants in Canada in 2015, 2016 and 2017 by OpenTable.

ABOUT THE CHEF

Kenny Kaechele entered the fine-dining world via legendary Mescalero, a popular drinking and dining spot in downtown Calgary. At age 24, he was head chef at The Living Room, where he caught the attention of Canadian Rocky Mountain Resorts (CRMR). He was chef de cuisine at CRMR's Divino Wine & Cheese Bistro and executive chef at The Ranche. After helping Concorde Group launch ei8ht, Kaechele shifted his attention toward opening his own restaurant and, by 2013, had struck a deal with the GRAND Theatre. And so WORKSHOP was born.

When Kenny Kaechele opened WORKSHOP Kitchen + Culture in September 2014, in the GRAND Theatre, his vision was to create a restaurant that paid homage to performing arts. Designer Connie Young created a warm, dark and moody space featuring two dining rooms and a chef's counter in front of the open kitchen; a second-floor bar serves primarily as a private dining and event space. The dinner menu changes daily and features excellent three- and five-course "improv" menus. The ever-changing three-course Lougheed Lunch is served in under an hour—ideal for fast-moving corporate Calgary. WORKSHOP also hosts events and

Black garlic aioli

1½ cups mayonnaise

1 Tbsp grainy mustard or pickled mustard seeds

1 tsp sherry vinegar

Small pinch of red chili flakes

4 cloves black garlic, mashed

Pecorino crumble

2 ciabatta buns, torn into small pieces

½ cup grated pecorino or Parmesan

2 Tbsp extra-virgin olive oil

Roasted cipollini onion

2 cipollini onions, trimmed and peeled

1 to 2 tsp olive oil

Lamb tartare

8 oz fresh lamb sirloin, finely chopped

¼ bunch Italian parsley, chopped, plus extra for garnish

Roasted Cipollini (see here)

1½ Tbsp Black Garlic Aioli (see here)

1 Tbsp extra-virgin olive oil

Assembly

Maldon salt

Freshly ground black pepper, to taste

¼ cup Pecorino Crumble (see here)

Parsley, microgreens or watercress, for garnish

Lamb Tartare with Black Garlic Aioli, Charred Cipollini and Pecorino Crumble

Serves 4

This innovative dish is a complete meal in itself. Chef Kenny Kaechele rejuvenated a traditional recipe by mixing ground lamb sirloin with black garlic aioli, then topping it with a pecorino-ciabatta crumble, which acts as the bread component. The key is to use good-quality fresh lamb.

Black garlic aioli In a small bowl, mix together all ingredients to combine. Set aside. (Leftover aioli can be stored in an airtight container in the refrigerator for up to 1 week. It can be used in sandwiches and vegetarian trays, or as the rouille in bouillabaisse.)

Pecorino crumble Preheat oven to 400°F.

Place ciabatta on a baking sheet and bake for 10 minutes, or until dried out.

On a separate baking sheet lined with parchment paper, spread out pecorino (or Parmesan) and bake for 8 to 10 minutes, until melted and slightly golden. Set aside to cool.

In a food processor, process cheese, ciabatta and oil until crumbled. Reduce oven temperature to 350°F.

Roasted cipollini onion Cover onions in oil, then wrap in aluminum foil and bake for 15 minutes. Remove from the oven, cool and cut into wedges.

Lamb tartare In a bowl, combine lamb, parsley, roasted cipollini, black garlic aioli and oil and gently mix until fully incorporated. (Do not overmix.)

Assembly Spoon tartare onto individual plates, forming loose mounds. Season with salt and pepper. Sprinkle generously with pecorino crumble and garnish with parsley (or microgreens or watercress). Serve immediately.

Dukkah

2 Tbsp sesame seeds

2 Tbsp sunflower seeds

2 Tbsp pumpkin seeds

2 Tbsp fennel seeds

2 Tbsp coriander seeds

2 Tbsp cumin seeds

½ tsp cayenne pepper

1 tsp mild smoked paprika

Fried cauliflower

2 cups grapeseed oil or any other high-heat oil, such as canola, sunflower or peanut

1 head cauliflower, cut into bite-sized florets

Green olive tapenade

1 cup green olives stuffed with pimento and garlic, in oil

½ bunch Italian parsley, leaves only

¼ cup extra-virgin olive oil

1 Tbsp capers

Harissa aioli

½ cup mayonnaise

2 tsp cumin seeds, toasted and crushed

2 tsp fennel seeds, toasted and crushed

1 tsp mild smoked paprika

½ tsp coriander seeds, toasted and crushed

½ tsp garlic powder

½ tsp kosher salt, plus extra to taste

Pinch of cayenne pepper

Grated zest and juice of 1 lime, plus extra to taste

Assembly

Pinch of kosher salt

Cilantro, for garnish

Dukkah-Fried Cauliflower with Green Olive and Harissa Aioli

Serves 4

The expression "If it ain't broke, don't fix it" applies to this signature WORKSHOP recipe, which has been on the menu since day one. Hearty, healthy and packed with flavour, this vegetarian dish is a customer favourite.

Dukkah Preheat oven to 350°F. Line a baking sheet with parchment paper.

Place sesame, sunflower and pumpkin seeds on the prepared baking sheet and toast for 10 minutes. (Be sure to keep an eye on them so they don't burn.) Set aside to cool slightly. Reduce the oven temperature to 275°F.

In a food processor, pulse toasted seeds to a coarse grind. Spread them out on a baking sheet and dry in the warm oven for 30 minutes.

In a spice grinder, grind fennel, coriander and cumin seeds to a powder. (Alternatively, use a pestle and mortar.)

Combine the dried seeds, ground spices, cayenne pepper and smoked paprika. Set aside.

Fried cauliflower Heat oil in a deep-fryer to a temperature of 350°F.

Dry cauliflower completely. Working in batches, carefully lower cauliflower into the deep-fryer and cook for 5 to 8 minutes, until golden brown. Using a spider or slotted spoon, transfer cauliflower to a plate lined with paper towel. Repeat with the remaining cauliflower. (Alternatively, for a healthier option, toss the cauliflower in oil and roast in a 420°F oven for 20 to 25 minutes, until tender and browned.)

Green olive tapenade In a food processor, pulse all ingredients until chunky-smooth.

Harissa aioli In a bowl, whisk together all ingredients. Adjust seasonings to taste with more salt or lime juice. (Leftover aioli can be stored in an airtight container in the refrigerator for up to 2 weeks.)

Assembly In a bowl, toss cauliflower, dukkah, green olive tapenade and a pinch of salt. (Be careful not to over-season, as the tapenade provides ample saltiness.) Spoon harissa aioli onto a serving platter, then arrange cauliflower overtop. Garnish with cilantro and serve family-style.

Yellow Door Bistro

Quinn Staple and Scott Redekopp

Over the years, the culinary team has participated in prominent events, including Cook It Raw Alberta and the Harvest Moon Gala. In 2018, Yellow Door Bistro won Best Small Plate at the Chef Meets BC Grape event.

ABOUT THE CHEFS

For chef de cuisine Scott Redekopp (pictured), breakfast is not only the most important meal of the day, it's also a career choice. Born in Saskatoon, Redekopp was influenced by his parents at an early age: his mother baked homemade croissants and his dad loved whipping up midweek meals from scratch. Redekopp travelled to Italy in his teens and learned about making quality food with simple ingredients.

He completed his Red Seal certification at SAIT (Southern Alberta Institute of Technology) and eventually opened Yellow Door Bistro as morning chef de partie. Redekopp's efforts didn't go unnoticed—in 2013, his pancakes were featured on Food Network Canada. As the current chef de cuisine at Yellow Door, he serves up every breakfast and brunch with confidence. "For our guests, this is the most influential meal of the day, and this is what they'll remember."

For executive chef Quinn Staple, see Oxbow (p. 152).

Yellow Door Bistro has staked its place in Calgary's thriving restaurant scene. Located in the Hotel Arts building, this award-winning restaurant uses quality, seasonal ingredients to create unique bistro-style fare.

Executive chef Quinn Staple played an instrumental role in opening Yellow Door Bistro back in 2013. His menu highlights a fresh take on a lighter style of French cuisine.

The menu features gluten-free options and drink specials throughout the week, as well as a weekday Happy Hour. The dining room's design combines classical and contemporary elements with plenty of comfortable banquette seating and warm lighting for a contemporary dining experience. What this means is that whether you are a hotel guest or just want dinner and a drink in a beautiful room, come in and pull up a chair.

Pickled red onion
½ cup apple cider vinegar
1 Tbsp granulated sugar
1 tsp pickling spice
1 tsp kosher salt
1 red onion, thinly sliced

Buttermilk-dill dressing
½ cup buttermilk
¼ cup sour cream
¼ cup mayonnaise
2 Tbsp finely chopped dill
1 Tbsp red wine vinegar
1 tsp kosher salt
½ tsp freshly ground black pepper

Five-minute egg
1 Tbsp baking powder
4 eggs, room temperature

Cobb salad
1 head iceberg lettuce, trimmed and
    cut into 4 (1-inch-thick) rounds
Buttermilk-Dill Dressing (see here)
Pickled Red Onion (see here)
1 avocado, chopped
12 cherry tomatoes, halved
¼ cup crumbled blue cheese
1 Tbsp finely chopped chives
4 Five-Minute Eggs (see here)
Kosher salt and freshly ground black
    pepper, to taste

Serves 4

Cobb Salad

This American classic is really a main course, and the Yellow Door Bistro's version of the salad is no exception. So filling, so good!

Pickled red onion In a small saucepan, combine vinegar, sugar, pickling spice and salt and bring to a boil.

Put onion in a bowl. Strain the pickling liquid into the bowl, then chill mixture in the refrigerator.

Buttermilk-dill dressing In a bowl, combine all ingredients. Keep in the refrigerator until ready to use.

Five-minute egg Bring a small saucepan of water to a boil. Stir in baking powder. (This will make peeling the eggs much easier.) Be careful, as the water will foam briefly.

Carefully lower eggs into the water and cook for 5 minutes and 30 seconds. Meanwhile, fill a bowl with ice water. Transfer cooked eggs to the ice bath and chill. Carefully peel eggs and store in a bowl of water in the refrigerator until needed.

Cobb salad Place a round of lettuce on each of four plates. Drizzle a generous amount of buttermilk-dill dressing over each round.

In a bowl, mix together pickled onion, avocado, tomatoes, blue cheese and chives. Spoon mixture overtop the dressed lettuce rounds. Create a nest in the centre of the pickled onion garnish and place an egg on top. Season with salt and pepper and serve.

Lemon-ricotta pancake batter

1 cup all-purpose flour
3 Tbsp icing sugar
2 tsp granulated sugar
2 tsp baking powder
¼ tsp kosher salt
1 cup full-fat buttermilk,
   plus extra if needed
½ cup ricotta
3 Tbsp melted butter
3 Tbsp condensed milk
2 large eggs
1 tsp vanilla extract
Grated zest and juice of 2 lemons

Lemon curd

Grated zest and juice of 4 lemons
½ cup (1 stick) unsalted butter,
   cut into ½-inch cubes
3 large eggs
3 egg yolks
¾ cup granulated sugar
¼ tsp kosher salt

Meringue

1 cup granulated sugar
4 fresh egg whites
1 tsp cream of tartar

Assembly

Unsalted butter, for greasing
Edible flowers, for garnish
   (optional)

Serves 4

Lemon-Ricotta Pancakes

You won't want to wait for a special occasion to make these rich, not-too-sweet pancakes. Topped with lemon curd and meringue, now that's how to start the day!

Lemon-ricotta pancake batter In a bowl, combine flour, both sugars, baking powder and salt.

In a separate bowl, combine the remaining ingredients. Slowly stir the wet ingredients into the dry ingredients until batter is smooth (some small lumps are okay). Add more buttermilk, if needed, to get the right consistency.

Lemon curd Fill a large bowl with ice water and place another bowl on top, with a strainer placed on the top bowl.

In a small saucepan, combine all ingredients. Bring to a simmer over medium-low heat, stirring continuously. Cook for another 2 minutes, stirring continuously to prevent eggs from scrambling. Remove from heat and strain into the bowl set over the ice water. Stir curd until chilled, then set aside in the refrigerator.

Meringue In a small saucepan, combine sugar and ½ cup water and heat over medium heat until sugar is dissolved and the temperature reaches 239°F.

Meanwhile, in a stand mixer fitted with the whisk attachment, slowly mix egg whites and cream of tartar to soft peaks.

Slowly and carefully pour sugar water into the egg whites and immediately whip on high speed until the meringue is fluffy and room temperature. Transfer meringue to a piping bag fitted with a 1-inch tip.

Assembly Preheat a griddle to 350°F and grease with butter.

Drop spoonfuls of pancake batter onto the griddle. Cook for 8 to 10 minutes, until tiny bubbles form on the surface. Flip, then cook until golden brown. Transfer to a plate to keep warm. Repeat with the remaining batter.

Divide pancakes among four plates, place a generous spoonful of curd on each and pipe meringue as whimsically and theatrically (or not) as you'd like onto the plate. Garnish with edible flowers, if using. Serve immediately.

Metric Conversion Chart

Volume

Imperial	Metric
⅛ tsp	0.5 mL
¼ tsp	1 mL
½ tsp	2.5 mL
¾ tsp	4 mL
1 tsp	5 mL
½ Tbsp	8 mL
1 Tbsp	15 mL
1½ Tbsp	23 mL
2 Tbsp	30 mL
¼ cup	60 mL
⅓ cup	80 mL
½ cup	125 mL
⅔ cup	165 mL
¾ cup	185 mL
1 cup	250 mL
1¼ cups	310 mL
1⅓ cups	330 mL
1½ cups	375 mL
1⅔ cups	415 mL
1¾ cups	435 mL
2 cups	500 mL
2¼ cups	560 mL
2⅓ cups	580 mL
2½ cups	625 mL
2¾ cups	690 mL
3 cups	750 mL
4 cups / 1 quart	1 L
5 cups	1.25 L
6 cups	1.5 L
7 cups	1.75 L
8 cups	2 L
12 cups	3 L

Weight

Imperial	Metric
½ oz	15 g
1 oz	30 g
2 oz	60 g
3 oz	85 g
4 oz (¼ lb)	115 g
5 oz	140 g
6 oz	170 g
7 oz	200 g
8 oz (½ lb)	225 g
9 oz	255 g
10 oz	285 g
11 oz	310 g
12 oz (¾ lb)	340 g
13 oz	370 g
14 oz	400 g
15 oz	425 g
16 oz (1 lb)	450 g
1¼ lbs	570 g
1½ lbs	670 g
2 lbs	900 g
3 lbs	1.4 kg
4 lbs	1.8 kg
5 lbs	2.3 kg
6 lbs	2.7 kg

Linear

Imperial	Metric
⅛ inch	3 mm
¼ inch	6 mm
½ inch	12 mm
¾ inch	2 cm
1 inch	2.5 cm
1¼ inches	3 cm
1½ inches	3.5 cm
1¾ inches	4.5 cm
2 inches	5 cm
2½ inches	6.5 cm
3 inches	7.5 cm
4 inches	10 cm
5 inches	12.5 cm
6 inches	15 cm
7 inches	18 cm
10 inches	25 cm
12 inches (1 foot)	30 cm
13 inches	33 cm
16 inches	41 cm
18 inches	46 cm
24 inches (2 feet)	60 cm
28 inches	70 cm
30 inches	75 cm
6 feet	1.8 m

Liquid measures (for alcohol)

Imperial	Metric
½ fl oz	15 mL
1 fl oz	30 mL
2 fl oz	60 mL
3 fl oz	90 mL
4 fl oz	120 mL

Cans and jars

Imperial	Metric
6 oz	170 mL
14 oz	398 mL
19 oz	540 mL
28 oz	796 mL

Baking pans

Imperial	Metric
5- × 9-inch loaf pan	2 L loaf pan
9- × 13-inch cake pan	4 L cake pan
11- × 17-inch baking sheet	30 × 45 cm baking sheet

Temperature

Imperial	Metric
90°F	32°C
120°F	49°C
125°F	52°C
130°F	54°C
140°F	60°C
150°F	66°C
155°F	68°C
160°F	71°C
165°F	74°C
170°F	77°C
175°F	80°C
180°F	82°C
190°F	88°C
200°F	93°C
240°F	116°C
250°F	121°C
300°F	149°C
325°F	163°C
350°F	177°C
360°F	182°C
375°F	191°C

Oven temperature

Imperial	Metric
200°F	95°C
250°F	120°C
275°F	135°C
300°F	150°C
325°F	160°C
350°F	180°C
375°F	190°C
400°F	200°C
425°F	220°C
450°F	230°C
500°F	260°C
550°F	290°C

Acknowledgments

While we may be the authors of the cookbook, great things are never done alone but require a team of good people. *Calgary Eats* was made possible with the guidance, support, and appetites of many.

We'd like to thank our publishing team: Chris Labonté, who initially pitched us the idea, and Michelle Meade, for editing with brevity and wit. Thank you to Judy Phillips and Breanne MacDonald for your eagle eyes, making sure all i's were dotted and t's crossed. Thank you to the creative director, Jessica Sullivan, who, along with photographer Chris Amat and stylist Kaitlin Moerman, made the book more beautiful and creative than we could have ever imagined. Thank you to everyone at Workshop Studios who provided ceramics: Becky McMaster, Claire Becq, Crystal Bennett, Quin Cheung, Chloe Collins, Tara Hadi, Chase Key, Shannon MacNaughton, Alexa Murray, Maggie Murray, Steph Schlachter, Lindsey Sheppard, Lauren Strybos, Tina Vidak and Natalie Wurz. As well, thank you to textile artist Irene Rasetti for the linens, Small Flower Floral Studio for the flowers and Kit Interior Objects for the Carl Hansen & Søn dining chair.

We'd also like to extend our gratitude to others who helped us along the way: Jane McCullough, for her astute editorial observations, and Regan Johnson, for her technical support. Thank you to Trisha Beavers, Sarah Boucher, Melissa Gorsedin, Karen Kho and Naomi Wyse for your help and advice at the chaotic recipe-testing dinners and for bringing the wine! A huge thank-you to Ian Grant for running out to pick up forgotten ingredients and for his unflagging support of the project.

We would also like to acknowledge each other: for our determination and strong friendship that saw this project through to its delicious conclusion.

Calgary Eats is defined by the chefs and restaurants whose vision and hard work continue to push boundaries and define Calgary's food scene. So, most importantly, thank you to all of you for your generosity in providing the recipes and your patience with our many questions, but, most of all, for your contributions to Calgary's flourishing dining scene.

Index

About
the Authors

GAIL NORTON

Gail Norton is the co-owner of Calgary's culinary hub The Cookbook Co. Cooks, a specialty cookbook, food and kitchenware store and cooking school. A lifelong Calgarian with deep and sprawling roots in the local food community, Norton is the former publisher of *City Palate* magazine, a judge for Taste Canada and co-author of four cookbooks: *Calgary Cooks, Dishing, Double Dishing* and *Cooks in My Kitchen*. She lives in Calgary.

KAREN RALPH

Karen Ralph moved to Calgary in 1979 and earned a BFA from Alberta College of Art and Design (ACAD). A freelance writer, she is also a food and wine instructor at The Cookbook Co. Cooks and organizer of the wine tours for its annual food and wine camps in the south of France (she has travelled to France 22 times—and counting). As well, she is a long-time contributor to *City Palate*, a self-titled roving ambassador for Metrovino, and co-author of *Calgary Cooks*. A lover of food, wine and cooking, Ralph lives in Calgary.